I SCREAM, YOU SCREAM,
WE ALL SCREAM
BECAUSE PUNS SUCK

Other *Pearls Before Swine* Collections

Stephan's Web
I'm Only in This for Me
King of the Comics
Breaking Stephan
Rat's Wars
Unsportsmanlike Conduct
Because Sometimes You Just Gotta Draw a Cover with Your Left Hand
Larry in Wonderland
When Pigs Fly
50,000,000 Pearls Fans Can't Be Wrong
The Saturday Evening Pearls
Macho Macho Animals
The Sopratos
Da Brudderhood of Zeeba Zeeba Eata
The Ratvolution Will Not Be Televised
Nighthogs
This Little Piggy Stayed Home
BLTs Taste So Darn Good

Treasuries

Pearls Hogs the Road
Pearls Gets Sacrificed
Pearls Falls Fast
Pearls Freaks the #%# Out*
Pearls Blows Up
Pearls Sells Out
The Crass Menagerie
Lions and Tigers and Crocs, Oh My!
Sgt. Piggy's Lonely Hearts Club Comic

Gift Books

Friends Should Know When They're Not Wanted
Da Crockydile Book o' Frendsheep

AMP! Comics for Kids

Suit Your Selfie
When Crocs Fly
Skip School, Fly to Space
The Croc Ate My Homework
Beginning Pearls

I SCREAM, YOU SCREAM, WE ALL SCREAM BECAUSE PUNS SUCK

A PEARLS BEFORE SWINE COLLECTION

BY STEPHAN PASTIS

Introduction

I'm often asked at book signings if my strips are simply presented to me, fully formed, like grapes from the gods.

Actually, no one has ever asked me that.

Though I wish one of you would.

The truth is that it is a two-step process.

Step 1 involves a Post-it or loose scrap of paper. Here are four that are next to my desk right now:

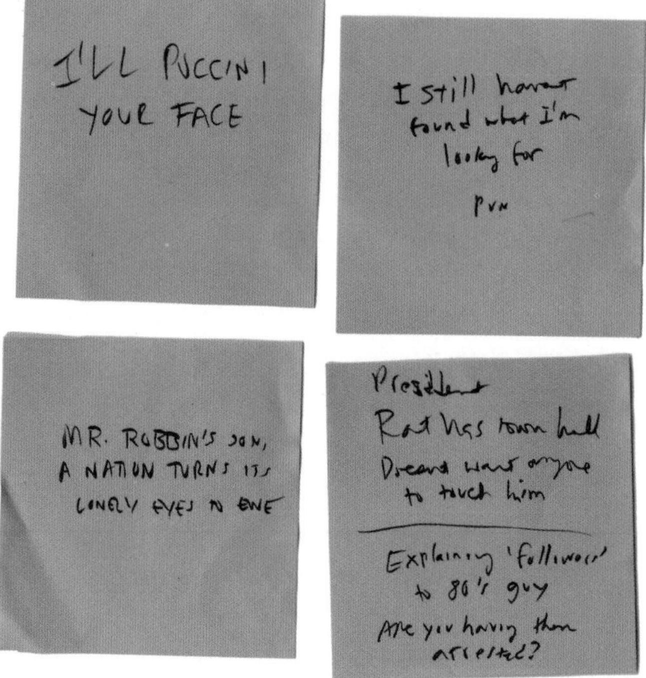

These are mere whiffs of an idea. Just semi-funny or interesting thoughts that strike me while reading, or listening to music, or doing nothing at all. So I write them down on little Post-its.

About half of them will become actual strips. The others will die sad and lonesome.

Clockwise, I can see that I'm playing around with the opera composer Puccini's name; U2's song "I Still Haven't Found What I'm Looking For"; a strip where Rat is president (and a second idea about a guy from the 80's); and then another pun strip, this one based on the Simon and Garfunkel song, "Mrs. Robinson."

Then when I go to write, I take out these notes and see if I can actually do anything with them. On good days, I can. On bad days, I can't. That part is rather unpredictable.

Over the years, I've learned that I can't write when I'm sick. Though I can write when I'm tired.

And when I'm sick *and* tired, I call John Glynn, the head of my syndicate, and complain. (Though he's gotten smart. My calls now go straight to voicemail.)

But having the notes is a comfort. Much better than staring at a blank page.

Step 2 is the heavy lifting. That's when I get out a notepad and try to work one of the Post-it notes into a strip. One that won't embarrass my friends and family.

Well, that's not true.

Everything I do embarrasses my family.

And I don't worry about my friends. Mostly because I don't have any.

I used to, like *Baby Blues* co-creator Rick Kirkman. But then I took up twenty minutes of his answering machine singing "Ol' Man River." (Of which I only know two lines, "Ol' Man River, that ol' man river.")

He didn't appreciate that.

Then there was my former friend, Mark Tatulli, creator of the comic strip *Lio*. I once called and left nine consecutive messages on his iPhone at midnight.

Each was four minutes long. Exactly four minutes. I know that because that's when his iPhone would cut me off.

Each of the messages was in the form of a radio show, with me as the host. I would take calls from listeners (also me), each one of whom would rip on Mark's cartooning abilities and personal life. One caller accused him of inappropriately fondling an 80-year-old cartoonist at a comic convention.

Okay, where was I?

Oh yeah, the writing stuff.

So sometimes (though rarely), Step 2 can be easy. The ideas just pour out ready to eat, like instant oatmeal (Don't know if this is apt. I've never had instant oatmeal).

Below is an example of an easy Step 2:

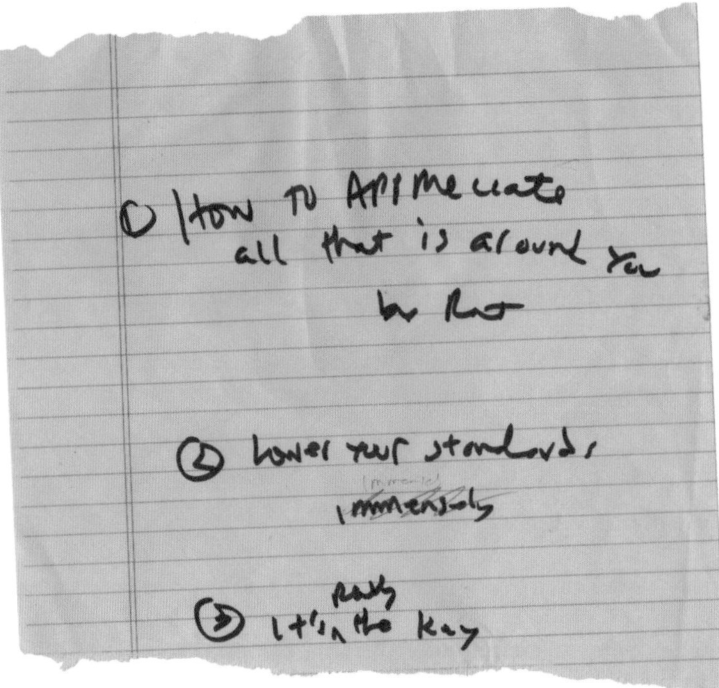

If you look at the strip it became (below), you'll see it's more or less the final strip (but for the last line):

But that's not typical.

Typical is the monstrosity on the next page.

Which looks less like grapes from the gods, and more like something police would find scribbled on the back of a paper bag in a drug shelter.

I can see from just looking at it that I had an idea that I liked: "losing with Grace." As in the person's name. But I couldn't get it right. So I took numerous stabs at it.

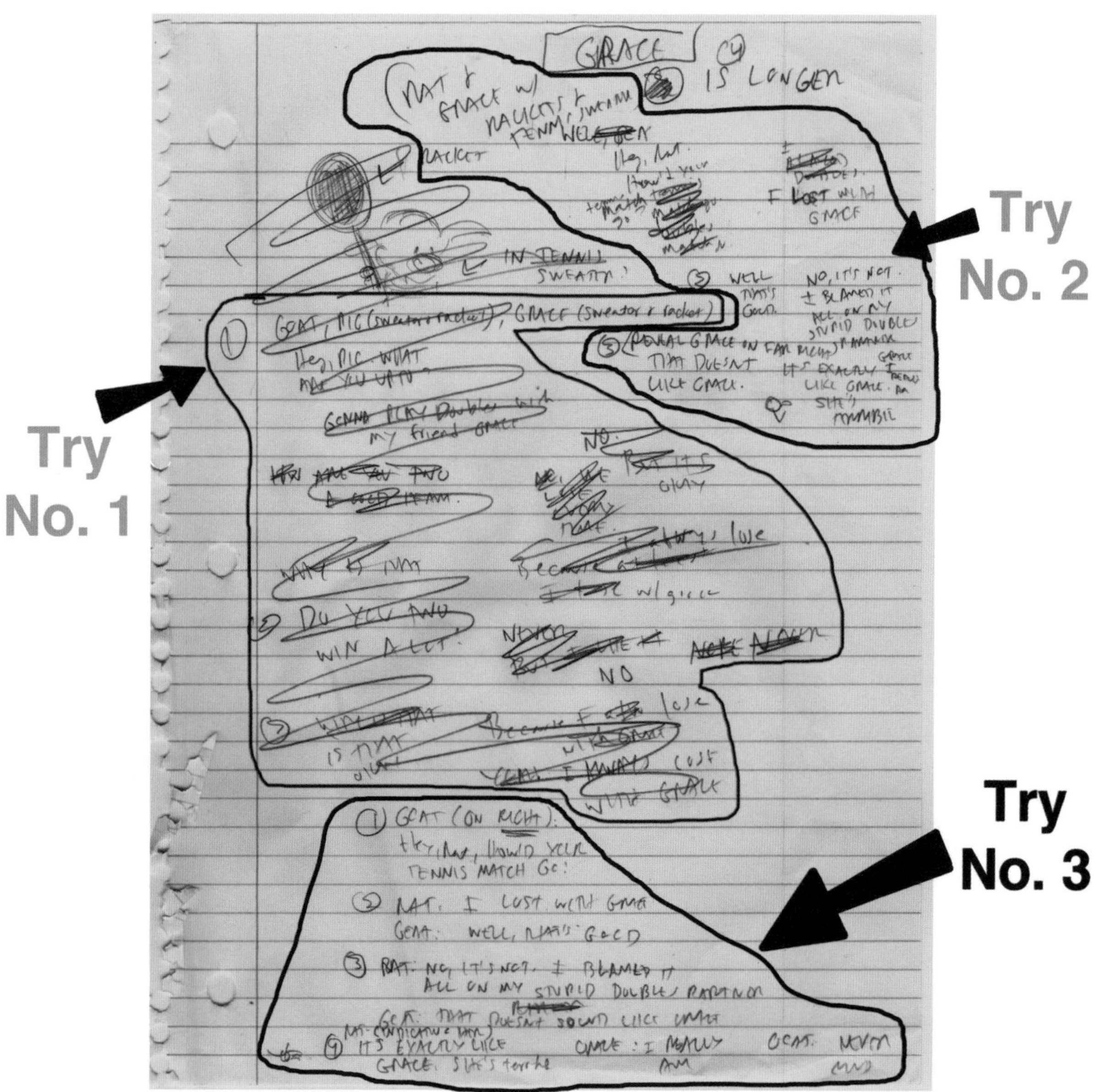

Try No. 3 is the one that became the actual strip. But it was preceded by many false starts, a lot of cross-outs, and at least one whiny call to John Glynn.

But below is the strip that the notes became.

And that, my friends, is the whole, ugly process. Minus the herbal tea and incense and music, which is best left for another intro.

It is a process that will leave you scorned by friends. Bereft of family.

But gloriously famous.

How famous? Famous enough that you can make any claim you want in a book intro.

Sincerely,

Stephan Pastis
Receiver of Grapes from Gods
September 2017

To Donna Oatney, the magician who makes
the covers of these books look as good as they do.

LOOK AT ME, GOAT... I'VE BECOME A JUDGE. IT'S ALWAYS BEEN A LIFE-LONG DREAM OF MINE.
JUDGE
RAT

GOOD FOR YOU, RAT. THAT'S A CRITICAL ROLE IN OUR SYSTEM OF DUE PROCESS. WHAT MADE YOU WANT TO DO IT?

THEY GIVE YOU A HAMMER TO HIT IDIOTS.
9/7

THAT'S NOT WHAT THAT'S FOR.
OKAY, YOU'RE FIRST.

HEY, RAT, WHAT ARE YOU DOING?
I'M A JUDGE NOW. I'M THE LIVING EMBODIMENT OF JUSTICE.

WHAT'S ON YOUR DESK THERE?
A TIP JAR. THE MORE YOU PUT IN IT, THE MORE JUSTICE-Y I FEEL.
9/8

SO *THAT'S* HOW JUSTICE WORKS.
YOU GET WHAT YOU PAY FOR.

I HEARD YOU HAD TO TEACH PIG ALL ABOUT WINE.
YEAH, HE'S GOING TO A FANCY RESTAURANT WITH PIGITA AND WANTS TO IMPRESS HER WITH HIS WINE KNOWLEDGE.

SO NOW HE KNOWS HOW TO ORDER A GOOD BOTTLE AND TASTE THE LITTLE SAMPLE THAT THE WAITER BRINGS YOU?
YEAH. THOUGH THERE'S JUST ONE LITTLE STEP I'M WORRIED ABOUT.
9/9

MUST YOU USE A SWIRLY STRAW?

JUDGE RAT IN SESSION. HOW CAN I HELP YOU?
YEAH. I SPILLED McDONALD'S COFFEE ON MYSELF AND IT WAS HOT. I'D LIKE TO RECEIVE JUST COMPENSATION.
JUDGE RAT
9/10

CRACK
JUDGE RAT

THAT SEEMS FAIR.
JUDGE RAT

JUDGE RAT IN SESSION. HOW CAN I HELP YOU?
YEAH. A REAL ESTATE AGENT SOLD ME A HOUSE WITH ALL SORTS OF PROBLEMS. I WAS WONDERING IF THERE WAS ANYTHING I COULD DO.
JUDGE RAT

YES. TAKE THE LAW INTO YOUR OWN HANDS.
JUDGE RAT
9/11

I CAN SOLVE ANYTHING.
JUDGE RAT

THERE'S A BIG DEBATE GOING ON AT MY CHURCH ABOUT A DRESS CODE. PEOPLE DON'T LIKE HOW CASUALLY SOME FOLKS NOW DRESS FOR SUNDAY SERVICES.
9/12

SO THEY WANT PEOPLE TO DRESS BETTER?
YEAH... AND THEY'RE TAKING SUGGESTIONS RIGHT NOW AT A BIG CHURCH MEETING.

SPANDEX! SPANDEX! SPANDEX!
SIT DOWN, JEF THE CYCLIST.

HEY, PIG, YOU HAVE TO HEAR THIS GREAT ELVIS SONG WITH ME.
CAN'T. I GOT A JOB WRITING HEADLINES FOR A NEWSPAPER AND THIS ONE STORY'S REAL TOUGH.

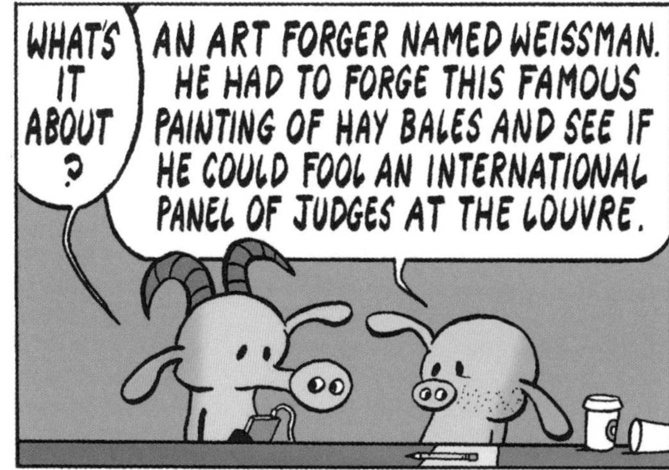
WHAT'S IT ABOUT?
AN ART FORGER NAMED WEISSMAN. HE HAD TO FORGE THIS FAMOUS PAINTING OF HAY BALES AND SEE IF HE COULD FOOL AN INTERNATIONAL PANEL OF JUDGES AT THE LOUVRE.

DID HE DO IT?
WELL, IT FOOLED THE RUSSIAN JUDGE, BUT THERE WAS A PROBLEM WITH THE AMERICAN JUDGE.

WHO WAS THE AMER-ICAN JUDGE?
HI FROM THE COMIC STRIP 'HI AND LOIS,' WHO INSISTED ON BRING-ING A FEMALE SHEEP TO THE JUDG-ING. AND THE TWO OF THEM KEPT FALLING ON THE LOUVRE FLOOR.

9/13

THAT'S NUTS. SO WHAT'S THE HEADLINE?

'WEISSMAN'S HAY ONLY FOOLS RUSSIAN,
BUT HI CAN'T HELP FALLING IN LOUVRE WITH EWE.'

WISE MEN SAY YOU'RE A SAD LITTLE MAN.

Okay, woomun...Me turn 47, but me still no leave mark een life. So me use savings estabeesh someting dat last.
YOU USED OUR SAVINGS? TO ESTABLISH WHAT? A BUSINESS? A CHARITY?

Larry
Me is da champeon
9/14

Ees much more sateesfying den charity.

JUDGE RAT IN SESSION
COUNSEL, LET ME TELL YOU RIGHT NOW. NO ONE LIKES TO HEAR A LAWYER TALK. SO KEEP YOUR SPEECHES SHORT, OR THIS COURT WILL CALL IN 'FRIENDLY KITTY.'
WHO IS FRIENDLY KITTY?
JUDGE
9/15

JUDGE

IT'S A BIT OF A MISNOMER.
JUDGE
RAT

Don't you ees hate guys come bar wid fancee jacket, fancee watch, like beeg show-off?
Oh, me so hate. Like, why you need show off?
9/16

Larry
Me is da champeon

You ees like beeg heepocrite, Larry.
Whoa. Who put dat dere?
Larry
Me is da champeon

HEY, RAT, WHAT HAPPENED TO YOUR JUDGE'S BENCH?
I TILTED IT TO SHOW THAT THE SCALES OF JUSTICE ARE NOT BALANCED IN MY COURTROOM, BUT ARE INSTEAD SUBJECT TO MY PREJUDICES AND WHIMSY.
JUDGE RAT

WHEEEEE
JUDGE RAT
9/17

WE SHOULD AVOID JUSTICE.
JUDGE RAT

WHAT DO YOU HAVE THERE, ZEBRA?
IT'S A GRANITE STONE I'VE INSTALLED AS A TRIBUTE TO ALL THE ZEBRAS KILLED BY CROCODILES. BUT I'M THINKING I MIGHT WANT TO MOVE IT.
IN MEMORY

WHY WOULD YOU MOVE IT? IT LOOKS PRETTY THERE.
IN MEMORY

Larry
Me is da champeon
IN MEMORY
9/18

MAYBE YOU SHOULD MOVE IT.
Hey, dat look like gud place rest my beer.
IN MEMORY

I'VE CONCLUDED THAT A CORPORATION IS A SOULLESS ENTITY DESIGNED SOLELY FOR THE ACCUMULATION OF MONEY, WITHOUT REGARD FOR THE EFFECT IT MAY HAVE ON HUMAN LIFE.

IF YOU FEEL SO STRONGLY, YOU SHOULD DO SOMETHING ABOUT IT.
YOU'RE RIGHT.

I'LL INCORPORATE.
9/19

PLEASE GET YOUR FOOT OFF MY HEAD.
LOOK...I'M PRACTICING STEPPING ON THE LITTLE GUY.

I AM NOT GOING TO HAVE TROUBLE SLEEPING TONIGHT.

I HAD SOME WARM MILK. I READ A RELAXING BOOK.

I HAVE THE ROOM TEMPERATURE PER-FECT. I HAVE A MASK FOR MY EYES.

I HAVE MY WHITE NOISE MAKER. I HAVE MY COMFY SHEETS.

AND NOW I CAN TURN OFF THE LIGHT AND GET A GOOD NIGHT'S SLEEP.

CLICK

9/20

WHO ARE YOU?

I'M THE GHOST OF ALL THE THINGS THAT CAN GO WRONG TOMORROW.

BUT I HAVE MY WARM MILK AND COMFY SHEETS.

IT'S GONNA BE A LONG NIGHT, ISN'T IT?
MOVE OVER. I HAVE LOTS TO TELL YOU.

HEY, GOAT. I'D LIKE YOU TO MEET MY FRIEND, TIMMY THE TORTOISE.
DOES HE COME OUT OF HIS SHELL?

NO.
WHY NOT?

HURT BY A GIRL IN '79.
9/21

HE'S TERRIBLE AT PARTIES.

SO, TIMMY THE TORTOISE, WHAT'S THE REAL REASON YOU DON'T COME OUT OF YOUR SHELL?
THE WORLD'S A DANGEROUS PLACE, AND IF I DON'T COME OUT OF MY SHELL, I CAN LIVE A LONG LIFE.

BUT WHAT'S THE POINT OF LIVING A LONG LIFE IF THE LIFE ITSELF IS SPENT IN A SHELL?

9/22

PARDON ME WHILE I EAT SOME LETTUCE AND CRY.

HOLA, PIG...YOU WANT ME TO THROW AWAY THIS 'MENTOS' WRAPPER?
ONE MOMENT, PEDRO... I'M ON THE PHONE.

QUÉ?
ONE MOMENT... I WANT TO KEEP IT... IT'S A REMINDER OF A SERIES OF GREAT DATES I'VE BEEN HAVING, AND I WANT TO KEEP THE GOOD LUCK GOING.

QUÉ?
UN MOMENTO... IT'S A MENTOS MOMENTUM MEMENTO.
9/23

TU ERES UN IDIOTA.

LISTEN, GOAT, I'VE TAKEN TO HEART WHAT YOU SAID ABOUT LEADING A MORE EXCITING, FULFILLING LIFE.

GOOD FOR YOU, TIMMY THE TORTOISE. HAVE YOU DECIDED TO FINALLY COME OUT OF YOUR SHELL AND SEE THE WORLD? MEET NEW PEOPLE? HAVE SOME ADVENTURES?

9/24

SATELLITE T.V. IS NOT—
PIPE DOWN. SPORTSCENTER'S ON.

I'M STAYING AT A CHARMING LITTLE BED AND BREAKFAST NEXT WEEK.
WHAT'S A BED AND BREAK-FAST?

WELL, THEY VARY, OF COURSE, BUT IN GENERAL, THEY'RE —

SOME WEIRDO'S HOUSE WHERE YOU EAT WITH STRANGERS AND SOMETIMES FIND THEM IN YOUR BATHROOM.
9/25

I NEED MY BATHROOM ALONE-TIME!
THEY'RE NOT IN YOUR BATH-ROOM.
IT'S LIKE HELL, BUT WITHOUT THE FLAMES.

WHAT ARE YOU DOING, RAT?
I GOT A JOB WRITING SCHOLARLY FILM CRITICISM. CHECK OUT MY FIRST MOVIE REVIEW.

Someone should hit the director with a stick.
9/26

I TAKE IT YOU DIDN'T LIKE IT.
I DUNNO. I HAVEN'T SEEN IT.

LONELY LINDY WAS LONELY.

SO SHE WENT ON FACEBOOK TO FIND OLD HIGH SCHOOL CLASSMATES.

AND LOOKED UP THE SKINNY DEBATE GEEK AND THE PIMPLY TUBA PLAYER AND THE SWEATY YEARBOOK EDITOR...

AND BROCK ROCKSON.

HIGH SCHOOL QUARTERBACK, BLOND-HAIRED STUD, AND MUSCLED ADONIS, BROCK'S PROFILE PHOTO WAS THE LOGO OF THE DETROIT LIONS.

'HE MUST HAVE GONE ON TO BE A PRO QUARTERBACK,' LINDY THOUGHT, AS SHE SENT BROCK A FACEBOOK MESSAGE.

'HI, I'M LINDY,' SHE SAID. 'I WENT TO HIGH SCHOOL WITH YOU. WOULD YOU EVER WANT TO GET COFFEE?' AND TO HER SURPRISE, BROCK SAID YES.

9/27

AND ON THE DAY OF THE MEETING, LINDY MADE HERSELF AS BEAUTIFUL AS POSSIBLE FOR HER HIGH SCHOOL ADONIS.

WHO SHOWED UP AN HOUR LATE.

SORRY. WAS GAMBLING ON THE PONIES. YOU LINDY?

LINDY DELETED HER FACEBOOK ACCOUNT AND SET FIRE TO HER COMPUTER.

DON'T LOOK BACK. SOMEONE MIGHT BE CHANGING ON YOU.

On a scale of zero to 100, how important is money to you?

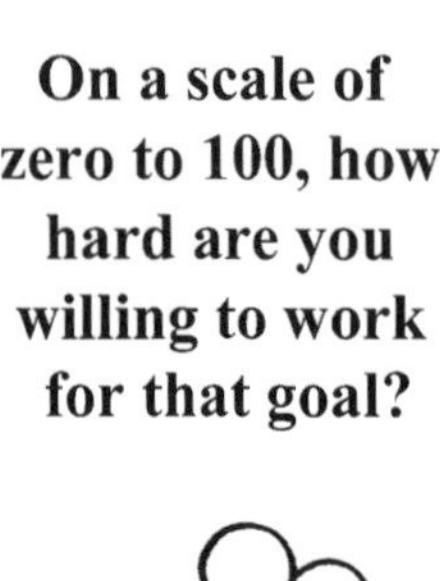

DO YOU KNOW ANY OF THE NINE JUSTICES ON THE SUPREME COURT?
ONE.

WHO?

DIANA ROSS.
10/1

SHE'S A SUPREME.
I KNOW. BUT I CAN'T NAME THE OTHER EIGHT.

DO YOU THINK IT'S TRUE THAT WHEN IT COMES TO RELATIONSHIPS, ABSENCE MAKES THE HEART GROW FONDER?
NO.

TOGETHERNESS MAKES THE HEART MORE ANNOYED.
10/2

NEVER WRITE GREETING CARDS.
THE KEY TO TOGETHERNESS IS NOT BEING TOGETHER.

HEY THERE, PIG...DID YOU HEAR I'M GONNA HAVE A SHOW OF MY WORK AT A CARTOON ART MUSEUM? NOW I JUST HAVE TO WRITE A BRIEF ARTIST'S STATEMENT EXPLAINING MY WORK AND OUTLINING MY ARTISTIC VISION.
HERE. TRY THIS.

I suck.
10/3

PERHAPS I'LL WRITE MY OWN.
IT IS BRIEF.
HANG ON... I WANT TO ADD SOME EXCLAMATION POINTS.

CAN I PLEASE TALK TO PIG?

THIS IS PIG.
HI, PIG... I HAVE YOUR TEST RESULTS.

OH MY GOODNESS. WHAT ARE THEY?
THEY'RE NEGATIVE.

OH, GAWD, NOOOOO... HOW MUCH TIME DO I HAVE LEFT?
RELAX, PIG. IT'S A POSITIVE THING.

NEGATIVE IS POSITIVE?
YES.

THEN WHAT'S A POSITIVE RESULT?
A NEGATIVE THING.

POSITIVE IS NEGATIVE?
YES.
10/4

ARE YOU SURE?
I'M POSITIVE.

OH, GAWD, NOOOOO... HOW MUCH TIME DO YOU HAVE LEFT?

NEXT TIME, YOU CALL HIM.
YOU LIVED A GOOD LIFE, DOC.

THE NEIGHBORHOOD ASSOCIATION WANTS TO CUT DOWN THIS TREE.
SO WHAT? IT'S A STUPID TREE.

I THINK IT'S A SPECIAL TREE.
OH, PLEASE. WHY IS IT ANY MORE SPECIAL THAN ANY OTHER TREE?

BECAUSE WHEN I SHAKE IT, MONEY FALLS OUT.
10/5

I'M A TREE-HUGGING HIPPIE.
I ♡ MOTHER EARTH

RAT AND PIG HAVE FOUND A MONEY TREE. RAT HAS SPENT 24 HOURS SHAKING IT.
YOU SHOULD COME IN NOW, RAT. YOU'VE BEEN OUT HERE FOREVER.
I WILL SHAKE THIS TREE 'TIL THE END OF @☆#@#@ TIME!

WELL, IT'S NICE TO SEE YOU SPENDING SO MUCH TIME IN NATURE. IT'S LIKE YOU'RE AN ENVIRONMENTALIST NOW. AND LOOK, THE TREE HAS A CUTE L'IL SQUIRREL!
10/6

TOUCH MY MONEY AND I'LL RIP YOUR LITTLE SQUIRREL ARMS OFF!!!

I DON'T THINK THE SIERRA CLUB WOULD APPROVE OF THAT.
HE'S STUFFING MONEY IN HIS CHEEKS! HE'S STUFFING MONEY IN HIS CHEEKS!

HEY, STEPH, WHAT HAPPENS IF YOU DRAW ME WITHOUT HORNS?
LIKE THIS?
10/7

YEAH, AND THEN MAYBE SHORTEN MY SNOUT AND MAYBE MAKE IT A LITTLE SMALLER.

YOU KNOW, SOME CARTOONISTS HAVE MORE THAN ONE CHARACTER DESIGN.
I KNOW!
HEY, STEPH, WHAT HAPPENS IF YOU ERASE MY STRIPES AND GIVE ME HORNS?

RAT AND PIG HAVE FOUND A MONEY TREE
OKAY, PIG, NOW THAT WE'VE FOUND THE MONEY TREE, WE HAVE TO GUARD AGAINST ANYONE ELSE FINDING IT, BUT IN A SMART, SUBTLE WAY THAT DOESN'T AROUSE SUSPICION.

HEY GUYS, WHAT ARE YOU — WHOA, IS THAT MONEY UP —

CRACK

REMEMBER — HE GOT HIT BY A VERY LARGE COCONUT.

CHECK IT OUT, GOAT...I'M MAKING BABY DOLLS FOR KIDS. IN FACT, I'M SELLING SO MANY I CAN'T KEEP UP AND DON'T KNOW WHAT TO DO.
ASK AROUND HERE AT THE CAFE. I'M SURE THERE ARE TONS OF PEOPLE WHO NEED WORK.

PARDON ME, MA'AM, BUT WOULD YOU LIKE TO MAKE BABIES WITH ME?

NO ONE NEEDS WORK.

AT WHAT POINT DOES A HOME REPAIR PROJECT BECOME TOO BIG AND TOO COMPLEX FOR YOU, SUCH THAT YOU FEEL THE NEED TO CALL IN A REPAIR PROFESSIONAL?

IF IT INVOLVES A HAMMER.

NOT THE HANDY TYPE?
OR IF THE BATTERY COVER FALLS OFF THE REMOTE.

WHY DO WE HAVE TO PASS A TEST TO DRIVE?
BECAUSE THERE ARE MANY RULES INVOLVED IN DRIVING.

AND DRIVERS HAVE TO BE KNOWLEDGABLE TO DO THAT?
OF COURSE.

AND WHO MAKES THE RULES OF THE ROAD?
GOVERNMENT OFFICIALS.

AND GOVERNMENT OFFICIALS HAVE TO BE KNOWLEDGABLE TO DO THAT?
OF COURSE.

AND WHO ELECTS THE GOVERNMENT OFFICIALS?
WE DO WHEN WE VOTE.

AND WE HAVE TO BE KNOWLEDGABLE TO DO THAT?

10/11

WE DON'T HAVE TO KNOW SQUAT!!

I LIKE TO FIND FLAWS IN THE SYSTEM.

BOOOOOO

WHAT DO YOU THINK YOU'RE DOING?
BOOING THIS PLAY. THE ACTING IS AMATEURISH, THE SINGING IS POOR, AND THE PRODUCTION VALUE IS NOT UP TO PAR.

IT'S A FIFTH GRADE SCHOOL PLAY.
10/12

I *THOUGHT* THEY WERE RATHER SHORT
BOOOOOO, SHORT PEOPLE!

I GOT A RECALL NOTICE.
WHAT ARE THEY RECALLING? YOUR CAR?

ME.
10/13

SOMETIMES IT'S JUST NOT YOUR YEAR.

HEY, PIG, THIS IS HAROLD. HE TEACHES A NUMBER OF LANGUAGES AT THE UNIVERSITY.
I SEE. WHAT LANGUAGES DO YOU ENJOY THE MOST?

WELL, AT SCHOOL, IT'S AXIOMATIC THAT MY TASTES CAN BE A BIT MERCURIAL AND ANTEDILUVIAN.
10/14

POMPOUSESE.

WHAT ARE YOU READING?
'KILLING PATTON' BY BILL O'REILLY.

INTERESTING. WHAT ARE SOME OF HIS OTHER WORKS?
'KILLING KENNEDY.' 'KILLING JESUS.' 'KILLING LINCOLN.'
10/15

I SENSE A THEME.
THE MAN HAS A GIFT!!

HEY, GOAT... WHAT DOES IT TAKE FOR A BOOK TO BECOME KNOWN AS GREAT LITERATURE?

IT HAS TO BOTH BORE AND CONFUSE EVERYONE.
10/16

NO.
EXCEPT FOR HIGH SCHOOL ENGLISH TEACHERS. THEY HAVE TO LIKE IT.
WHAT'S WRONG WITH THOSE PEOPLE?

I THINK I HAVE TO GIVE MY HAMSTER AWAY. I DON'T HAVE TIME TO CARE FOR IT ANYMORE.
SEND HIM TO THAT CITY IN EUROPE THAT THEY CONTROL.

WHAT ARE YOU TALKING ABOUT?
HAMSTERDAM.
10/17

AMSTERDAM. AND IT'S NOT FOR HAMSTERS.
THEN WHAT HOLDS BACK THE HAMSTER RIVER?

Angry Bob was angry.

"I will fly to Las Vegas and that will make me happy."

Near the end of the flight, the flight attendant made an announcement.

"We've begun our descent. But before we land, I thought we'd have some fun with a game I call, 'Get to Know Your Fellow Passengers.'"

"Here's how it works: One person will speak and say their favorite thing about this trip to Vegas. Then the next person will say hi to the previous person and say *their* favorite thing about this trip."

"I'll go first," said the flight attendant. "My name is Katy. I like the Vegas hotels." A flight attendant named Jack stood up next. "Hi, Katy. The casinos."

10/18

Angry Bob, excited by how much fun he was having on the flight, stood up next.

"Hi, Jack! This airplane!"

T.S.A. officials arrested Bob upon arrival.

I'M LEARNING HOW TO TURN WOOD INTO PAPER.
WHO'S TEACHING YOU?

A PRIEST. HE TEACHES ME RIGHT FROM THE PULPIT. AND HE USES VISUAL AIDS LIKE PUPPETS TO MAKE IT EASIER TO UNDERSTAND.
WHAT ARE YOU TWO TALKING ABOUT?

PIG'S A PULPIT PUPPET PULPING PUPIL.
10/19

I SHALL BEAT YOU TO A PULP.

HEY, GOAT. WHATCHA DOING TODAY?
HE'S TAKING A BATH WITH HUNDREDS OF MARGINALLY CLEAN STRANGERS.
10/20

I'M GOING SWIMMING AT THE PUBLIC POOL.

I THINK I SAID THAT.

WHERE'S RAT TODAY?
HOSTAGE NEGOTIATION CLASS. HE WANTS TO LEARN HOW THE POLICE DO IT.
10/21

WHAT DO THEY TEACH THEM?
WELL, I THINK THE FIRST CLASS IS JUST FINDING OUT HOW YOU'D NATURALLY REACT TO A FRIEND OF YOURS BEING TAKEN HOSTAGE.

WE NEVER LIKED HIM MUCH ANYWAYS!!
OKAY.. UH.. NOT IDEAL.

HI, PIG, THIS IS YOUR GIRLFRIEND PIGITA'S MOTHER. I HEAR SHE'S WEARING NEW CLOTHES AND I WANT TO KNOW WHAT YOU THINK.
WELL, I'M NOT INTO THE HATS SHE'S WEARING, AND I'M NOT INTO THE SHOES.
10/22

DO YOU LIKE ANY OF IT?
WELL, I'M STARTING TO GET INTO HER PANTS.

MY GIRLFRIEND'S MOTHER CAN BE TEMPERAMENTAL.

WHAT ARE YOU INSTALLING, RAT?
THIS NEW, ADVANCED SOFTWARE. IT ALLOWS ME TO GO ONLINE AND BUY BEER.
10/23

WHAT'S ADVANCED ABOUT THAT? YOU CAN GO ONLINE AND BUY ANYTHING.

I'M HOPING FOR A FREE NACHOS UPGRADE.

SOME PEOPLE BELIEVE THAT WHEN THEIR LOVED ONES DIE, THEIR SPIRITS INHABIT THE BODIES OF HOUSEHOLD PETS.
10/24

GET A JOB, YOU LAZY @☆#@.

GOOD OLD DAD.

DING
DONG
DING
DONG

HEY. NICE COSTUMES, RAT AND PIG.

PLEASE GIVE US CANDY, NEIGHBOR BOB.
OR WE'LL WRITE SOMETHING BAD ABOUT YOU ON TWITTER.

WRITE SOMETHING BAD ABOUT ME ON TWITTER? WHAT KIND OF HALLOWEEN GREETING IS THAT?

10/25

TRICK OR TWEET.

WE GOT MORE CANDY THAN EVER.
SOCIAL MEDIA IS THE KEY TO EXTORTION.

PARDON ME, SIR, BUT I'VE DECIDED TO SHIFT MY FOCUS TO AMPHIBIOUS OPERATIONS.
10/26

SO I'LL NEED YOUR ASSISTANCE IN PROCURING A SHELTERED WATERWAY, ONE THAT I CAN USE AS AN OPERATIONAL BASE.

I EXPECTED MORE.

HEY, PIG, CAN I USE YOUR BATHROOM? I GOTTA GO BAD.
SURE, STEPH, RIGHT IN THERE.

10/27

I THINK I'LL HOLD IT.

IN THE PAST, IF YOU HAD AN IMPORTANT IDEA YOU WANTED TO EXPRESS TO THE WORLD, YOU NEEDED A TYPEWRITER AND THE POST OFFICE AND AN AGENT AND A YEAR OF WAITING AND A PUBLISHER AND A CHAIN OF BOOKSTORES AND THEN MAYBE YOU GOT A REACTION.
AND NOW?
10/28

I'm eating sausage links.
TYPE TYPE TYPE TYPE TYPE

44 COMMENTS:
Honey248:
Sausage suxxxx
IB4everyone:
Sausige ROCKS!!!
DerekTCA161:
STOP KILLIN ANIMALS

LET'S GO BACK TO THE OLD WAY.

I HEARD YOUR L'IL GUARD DUCK JOINED THE NAVY.
YEAH. AND HE'S ALREADY INVOLVED IN HIS FIRST NAVAL ENGAGEMENT.

OH, NO. AGAINST WHOM?
SNUFFLES THE CAT. THE TWO OF THEM HAD A FALLING OUT.
10/29

IT'S NOT QUITE THE MONITOR AND THE MERRIMAC, IS IT?

HEARD YOU'RE SICK, STEPH. JUST RE-MEMBER—FEED A FEVER, STARVE A COLD.
I THOUGHT IT WAS 'FEED A COLD, STARVE A FEVER.'
10/30

I'M PRETTY SURE IT'S 'FEED A FEVER, STARVE A COLD.'
I HEARD IT'S 'FEED A BEAVER, STARVE A COD'?

I HEARD IT'S 'FEED TOM SEAVER, STARVE A-ROD.'
ENOUGH!
LET'S JUST STARVE STEPH ON PRINCIPLE.

WHATCHA READING, GOAT?
A WAR HISTORY. THIS CHAPTER IS ABOUT ALL THE CARPET BOMBING THAT OCCURRED.
10/31

SOMEONE MUST REALLY HATE CARPETS.

I'M GOING TO READ SILENTLY NOW.
WHO WAS FIGHTING—TWO INTERIOR DECORATORS?

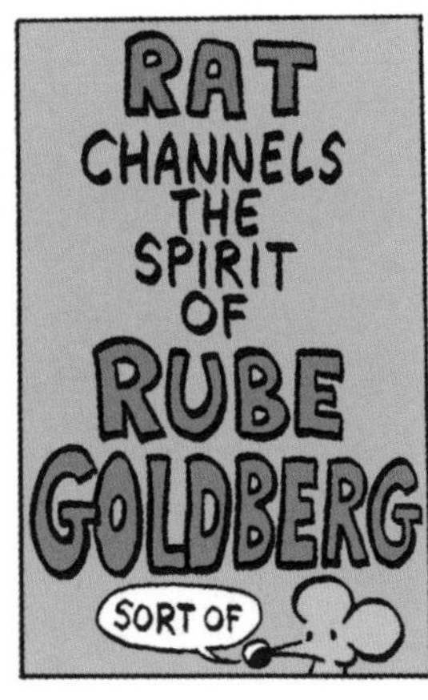

RAT
CHANNELS
THE
SPIRIT
OF
RUBE
GOLDBERG
SORT OF

Stephan (A) tells a bad pun that nobody likes.

Causing reader (B) to throw newspaper in disgust.

Hitting a random dog. (C)

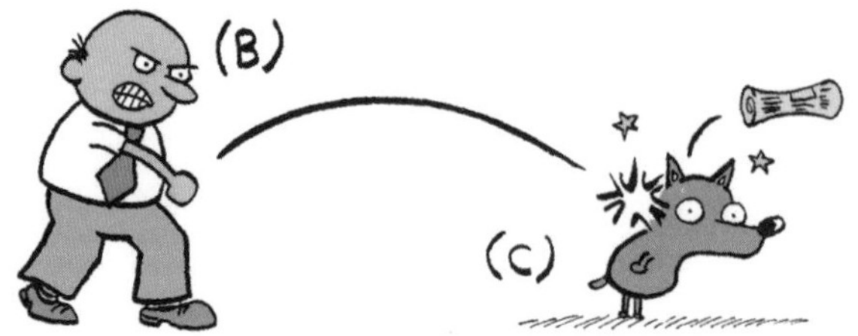

Who gets angry and bites the leg of a random flute player. (D)

Causing the flute to hit a very high note. (E)

That distracts two drivers (F), both named Burt, who crash into each other and die.

Which Stephan reads about in a newspaper, giving him an idea. (G)

About killing two Burts with one tone. (H)

11/1

YOU'RE NO RUBE.
YOU *ARE* A RUBE.
OW.

DO YOU THINK PEOPLE SHOULD HAVE TO KNOW BASIC INFORMATION ABOUT OUR GOVERNMENT BEFORE BEING ABLE TO VOTE?
OF COURSE NOT. THAT'S VERY ELITIST.

THIRTY-FIVE PERCENT OF AMERICANS CANNOT NAME A SINGLE BRANCH OF THE UNITED STATES GOVERNMENT.

OKAY, MAYBE A SMALL TEST.
OH, AND EIGHT PERCENT BELIEVE ELVIS IS ALIVE.
11/2

RAT IMPOSES 'SMART TEST' BEFORE VOTING
PARDON ME, SIR, BUT BEFORE VOTING, YOU NEED TO ANSWER A SIMPLE QUESTION ABOUT YOUR GOVERNMENT.
POLLING STATION
11/3

NO PROBLEM.
NAME JUST ONE JUSTICE OF THE U.S. SUPREME COURT.
POLLING STATION

HARRY CONNICK JR.
THAT'S 'AMERICAN IDOL.'
POLLING STATION

IS THERE A DIFFERENCE?
PLEASE, SIR, STEP AWAY FROM THE VOTING BOOTH.
POLLING STATION

SIR, THE MIDDLE EAST IS IN TURMOIL ONCE AGAIN. PERMISSION TO MOVE MY NAVAL FLEET TO THAT PART OF THE GLOBE?
WHATEVER YOU NEED, L'IL GUARD DUCK.

11/4

GOING TO THE BATHROOM JUST GOT A LOT LESS CONVENIENT.

HEY, EDDIE THE EAGLE. I HEARD YOU'RE THINKING OF MOVING TO EITHER CLEVELAND OR MIAMI. HAVE YOU MADE YOUR DECISION YET?
I HAVE.

WHAT IS IT?
I'M GONNA TAKE MY TALONS TO SOUTH BEACH.
11/5

WE'RE EJECTING YOU FROM THE COMIC STRIP.

PIG, I'D LIKE TO INTRODUCE YOU TO BOB. HE WORKS FOR THE D.O.D.
WHAT'S THE D.O.D.?
DEPARTMENT OF DEFENSE.

I'M A CATF. I WORK WITH THE CAAF AND THE CF ON THE DPI AND THE DCP FOR THE DOD IN ACCORD WITH NDS, NMCS, NIMS AND NDMS.
11/6

DOES HE SPEAK ENGLISH?
OMG. ROTFL.

HEY, PIG. WHY DIDN'T YOU MEET ME AT THE CAFE?
CAN'T TALK, GOAT. WE HAVE A SWAT TEAM CRAWLING ALL OVER THE HOUSE.

OH MY GOD, PIG...IS IT A HOSTAGE SITUATION?
I DON'T KNOW, BUT I CAN ASK.

ARE YOU TAKING THE FLY HOSTAGE?
BZZZZZZ
SWAT
SWAT
SWAT
11/7

NO.

WHAT ARE YOU DOING, RAT? IT'S TWO O'CLOCK IN THE MORNING.
I KNOW. THE WHOLE COUNTRY IS ASLEEP.

SO?
SO I'M GONNA CALL BOMBAST CABLE.

WHY?
BECAUSE EVERY TIME I NORMALLY CALL, A RECORDING TELLS ME THEY ARE EXPERIENCING AN 'UNUSUALLY HIGH CALL VOLUME.' BUT NOT NOW! NOT NOW, BABY! NOT AT TWO O' CLOCK IN THE G#@☆# MORNING!

Beep Beep Boop Beep Boop Beep Boop

Hello. We apologize for placing you on hold, but due to an unusually high call volume...

11/8

AAAAAAUGGGGGGGHHHHHHHH

I THINK I'LL GO BACK TO BED.
WHY DO YOU MOCK ME, BOMBAST? CAN'T WE JUST BE FRIENDS? PLEASE?

WE'RE GETTING CITED BY THE HOMEOWNERS ASSOCIATION FOR AN UNSIGHTLY FRONT YARD.
WHAT? I'VE BEEN MOWING THE LAWN WEEKLY.
11/9

I DON'T THINK IT'S THE LAWN.
WHAT ELSE COULD IT BE?

AHOY, MATEY.

WHAT ARE YOU DOING, RAT?
WRITING A NOVEL. BUT IT'S TOO HARD TO THINK OF IDEAS. TOO TAXING TO BE ORIGINAL.

SO WHAT ARE YOU GONNA DO?
FIND A JOB WHERE SOMEONE WILL PAY ME TO UTTER NOTHING BUT TRITE APHORISMS AND GLIB CLICHES.
AND WHO'S GONNA PAY YOU TO DO THAT?
11/10

GREAT GAME. DID YOU GIVE 110% OR WAS IT A TOTAL TEAM EFFORT?
34

RAT, THE SPORTS REPORTER
YOU HAD A GREAT GAME OUT THERE TODAY... TO WHAT DO YOU ATTRIBUTE THE VICTORY?
FIRST AND FOREMOST, TO GOD.
21
11/11

SO GOD WAS UP THERE ACTIVELY ROOTING AGAINST THE OTHER TEAM AND SLAMMING THE COFFEE TABLE WHEN THEY GOT A FIRST DOWN?
21

I SEE I'VE CONFUSED YOU.
21

RAT, THE SPORTS REPORTER
I'M HERE WITH OUR FOOTBALL ANALYST, TRENT. TRENT, WHAT'S THE KEY TO TODAY'S GAME?
RAT, THE KEY TODAY WILL BE SCORING POINTS.
11/12

GOOD, TRENT. SCORING POINTS SEEMS TO BE AN INTEGRAL PART OF WINNING A FOOTBALL GAME. WHICH RAISES ANOTHER QUESTION... DOES SOMEONE ACTUALLY PAY YOU FOR THIS?

THIS IS NOT GOING WELL.
SO, TRENT, WILL SHOWING UP FOR THE GAME BE ANOTHER KEY?

WHY DOES JEF THE CYCLIST ALWAYS HAVE TO WEAR SPANDEX?
I GUESS HE THINKS SPANDEX IS FLATTERING TO THE HUMAN BODY.

WELL, GUESS WHO TOOK UP CYCLING.
11/13

MY EYES CAN'T UN-SEE THAT.
IF ONLY STACI COULD SEE ME NOW.
ARE YOU CYCLING WITH CHILD?

DO YOU EVER WISH YOU HAD MORE FRIENDS?
WHAT FOR?

FRIENDS BROADEN YOUR KNOWLEDGE, TEACH YOU NEW STUFF, SHOW YOU AROUND NEW PLACES.

YOU JUST DESCRIBED GOOGLE.
11/14

SEARCH ENGINES AREN'T FRIENDS.
I'D SAY WE'RE BESTIES.

HELLO?

HEY, PIG... IT'S ME, GOAT... WHERE HAVE YOU BEEN? I HAVEN'T SEEN YOU IN A WHILE.

OH, GOAT... I'M SORRY. I THINK I'M JUST TRYING TO FIND MYSELF.

THAT'S NOTHING TO BE SORRY FOR, PIG. THAT SPIRITUAL JOURNEY IS THE PURPOSE OF LIFE!

IT IS?

SURE. SOME PEOPLE FIND IT THROUGH TRAVEL. SOME THROUGH READING. OR SPIRITUALITY. OR CRAFT.

11/15

BUT WHATEVER YOU DO, DON'T GET DISCOURAGED. SOMETIMES THAT SEARCH CAN TAKE YEARS.

THEN I'LL BE AT THE MALL A VERY LONG TIME.
1 2 3 4 5
YOU ARE HERE
7 8 9 10

I NEVER KNOW WHAT'S GOING ON.

WHY WOULD SOMEONE TRY TO GET SOMEONE ELSE DECLARED 'INCOMPETENT'?
WELL, SOMETIMES IT'S TO GET THAT PERSON'S MONEY AND GET THEM PUT INTO A MENTAL INSTITUTION.
11/16

OH.
WHY DO YOU ASK?

AND NOTE THE DUMB WAY HE WEARS HIS HAT.
LEMME GUESS... TWO AUTOGRAPH SEEKERS?

I HAVE A QUESTION ABOUT THE AMERICAN CIVIL WAR.
OH, GREAT... I LOVE HISTORY... IS YOUR QUESTION ABOUT GETTYSBURG? ROBERT E. LEE? APPOMATTOX?
11/17

WAS IT A WAR BETWEEN NORTH AND SOUTH DAKOTA?

LET'S START OVER.
BETWEEN NORTH AND SOUTH JERSEY?

I'M HAVING DINNER WITH A PROFESSOR FRIEND OF MINE TONIGHT. WANT TO COME ALONG?
WHAT'S YOUR FRIEND LIKE?
11/18

HE'S SORT OF THE ACADEMIC TYPE.
WHAT'S THAT MEAN?

IT MEANS HE BORES THE G☆#G OUT OF PEOPLE.

MAYBE I'LL EAT ALONE.
YOU WON'T REGRET IT.

DO YOU THINK A GIRL WOULD BREAK UP WITH ME JUST BECAUSE I'M NOT A GREAT KISSER?
OF COURSE NOT, PIG. BUT WHY? HOW DO YOU KISS?

11/19

NUTS. I DROOLED ON YOUR PANCAKE.
PLEASE NEVER DO THAT AGAIN.

CLICK
CLICK
CLICK
CLICK
CLICK
CLICK

SMACK
11/20

SELFIE STICKS HAVE MANY USES.

WHAT ARE YOU DOING, RAT?
HOLDING A BABY.
WHY?
11/21

OHHH...WHAT A CUTE BABY...YOU MUST BE A CARING, SENSITIVE MAN..HERE'S MY NUMBER...LET'S GET A DRINK SOME TIME.

A NEW LOW.
YOU CAN RENT THEM BY THE HOUR.
I WILL RENT A DOZEN!

HEY, GOAT, I'D LIKE YOU TO MEET MY BRITISH PAL, MR. DOWNS.
HI. HOW YOU DOING?
NOT WELL, LADS.

WHAT'S WRONG, DOWNS?
I'VE BEEN COOKING THIS ROAST IN A WOK, BUT MY WIFE DOESN'T LIKE IT.
WHY ARE YOU USING A WOK?

BECAUSE THAT'S HOW MY WIFE'S NAN USED TO DO IT.
WHAT'S A NAN?

THAT'S WHAT WE BRITS CALL OUR GRANDMA. AND EVER SINCE MY WIFE'S NAN DIED YEARS AGO, I'VE BEEN TRYING TO DO ALL THE THINGS SHE USED TO DO FOR MY WIFE.
TO TRY AND REPLACE HER NAN?

11/22

YEP. BUT AS MANY ROASTS AS I COOK IN THIS WOK, I GUESS IT JUST DOESN'T DO THE TRICK.

HOW MANY ROASTS MUST A MAN WOK, DOWNS, BEFORE THEY CALL HIM A NAN?

THE ANSWER, MY FRIEND, IS BLOWING UP THE CARTOONIST.

WHAT ARE YOU WRITING, RAT?
A KIDS BOOK. IT'S A LOT LIKE 'CURIOUS GEORGE,' BUT I TAKE IT A STEP FURTHER.
11/23

HOW DO YOU TAKE 'CURIOUS GEORGE' A STEP FURTHER?
BY MAKING HIM THIS...

Stalker George

KIDS BOOKS SHOULDN'T BE CREEPY.
I'M CHANGING THAT.

HEY, RAT...WANT TO MAKE THIS PUZZLE OF A KITTY KAT WITH US?
WHAT ARE YOU GONNA DO WITH IT WHEN YOU'RE DONE?

WHAT DO YOU MEAN? WE'LL JUST BREAK IT ALL UP AND PUT IT BACK IN THE BOX.
I SEE. SO IT'S AN ACKNOWLEDGMENT THAT OUR ROLE HERE ON EARTH IS SIMPLY TO PASS THE TIME UNTIL ONE DAY WE DIE.

WELL, I, FOR ONE, DON'T GIVE UP THAT EASY.
11/24

I JUST LIKE LOOKING AT KITTIES.

WHAT ARE YOU DOING, RAT?
WE HAVE ANTS. SO I'M GONNA SPRAY THEM WITH THIS ANT SPRAY.

DOES IT MAKE YOU FEEL BAD?
NO, BECAUSE ANTS DON'T SCREAM OR CALL FOR HELP, WHICH WE TAKE TO MEAN THEY DON'T SUFFER, WHICH ALLOWS US TO KILL THEM WITH IMPUNITY.
11/25

AHHHHHHHH!
LORDY, LORDY!
A DINGO TOOK MY BABY!

WELL, THAT WAS CREATIVE.
THOSE DARN DINGOS.

HEY, RAT, I'D LIKE TO INTRODUCE YOU TO OUR NEWEST CHARACTER... A WARTHOG.
HE'S JUST A PLAIN OLD WARTHOG?

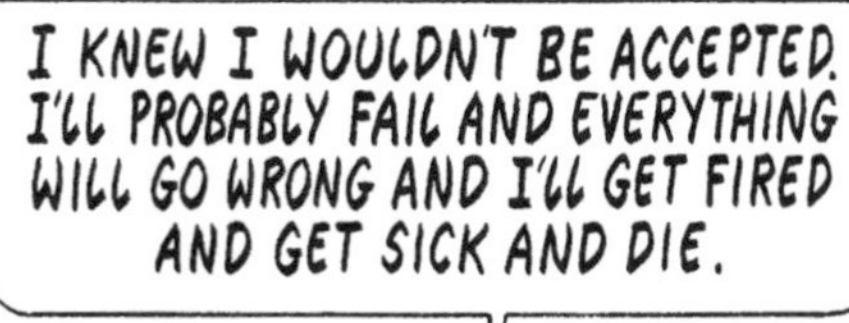
I KNEW I WOULDN'T BE ACCEPTED. I'LL PROBABLY FAIL AND EVERYTHING WILL GO WRONG AND I'LL GET FIRED AND GET SICK AND DIE.

A WORRYWARTHOG.
OH, GREAT... YOU'RE WHISPERING ABOUT ME... I'LL JUST FIRE MYSELF NOW.
11/26

IT SURE IS A BEAUTIFUL DAY... THE BIRDS, THE SUN... DON'T YOU JUST LOVE THE VIEW FROM THIS CLIFF, PIG?
11/27

CLIFFS CAN KILL YOU. SUNLIGHT CAN KILL YOU. BIRDS CAN KILL YOU.

NEXT TIME WE LEAVE THE WORRYWARTHOG AT HOME.
HOME? WHERE 77% OF ALL ACCIDENT-RELATED INJURIES OCCUR?

DO YOU THINK YOU'RE A HARD WORKER?
EVER HEARD OF THE PATH OF LEAST RESISTANCE?
11/28

YEAH.
THAT PATH'S TOO MUCH EFFORT FOR ME.

I SEE.
I PREFER THE PATH OF BEER AND SLEEP.

HEY THERE, GOAT...DID THE POWER OUTAGE AFFECT YOUR NEIGHBORHOOD YESTERDAY?
YEAH. NO WAY TO CHARGE MY MOBILE DEVICES OR ANYTHING.

OH MY. WHAT DID YOU DO?
I WENT OUTSIDE WITH SOME COFFEE AND JUST READ A NEWSPAPER.

THEN WHAT?
THEN I WENT TO MY LIBRARY AND GRABBED AN OLD BOOK, THE KIND WHERE THE PAGES HAVE THAT OLD MUSTY SMELL.

AND THEN WHAT?
THEN I WENT FOR A LONG WALK OUTSIDE WITHOUT ANY EMAIL TO CHECK OR G.P.S. TO GUIDE ME.

11/29

AND DID YOU GET LOST?
I DID. AND I HOPE TO DO IT AGAIN TOMORROW.

HE NEEDS HELP.

WHAT ARE YOU SELLING, PIG?
TURTLES WITH BROKEN LEGS. I'M HOPING THEY CAN FIND A CARING HOME WHERE THEY CAN REGAIN THEIR HEALTH.
FOR Sale

HOW MUCH DO THEY RUN?
THEY DON'T. THEY'RE TURTLES WITH BROKEN LEGS.
FOR Sale
11/30

I HATE STUPID QUESTIONS.
FOR Sale

HEY, CONNIE COW, WANT TO GO WITH ME TO NEIGHBOR BOB'S WEDDING? I DON'T HAVE A GUEST.
SURE. BUT MY UDDER IS SIGNIFICANTLY LARGER THAN NORMAL, SO I MAY BE UNCOMFORTABLE.

HEY, PIG, ARE YOU GOING TO NEIGHBOR BOB'S WEDDING WITH ANYONE?
YEAH. JUST CONNIE AND HER SIGNIFICANT UDDER.
12/1

NO WONDER YOUR WIFE LEFT YOU.

WHAT ARE YOU DOING, PIG?
I'M MAKING A STENCILED SIGN WELCOMING RAT HOME FROM HIS VACATION. BUT I DON'T HAVE AN 'R.'
12/2

DOES IT MAKE A DIFFERENCE?

WELCOME HOME, F IEND!

I GUESS NOT.

WHAT DO YOU HAVE THERE, RAT?
A GREAT TOY I INVENTED. IT'S A NEW TAKE ON THE JACK-IN-THE-BOX. CRANK THE HANDLE AND TRY IT.

DA DOO DA DOO DA DOODIDADOO DA DOO DA DOO DA DOOOO DOO
12/3

SPROING

DUCK-IN-A-BOX IS NOT A GOOD TOY.
'TOYS R US,' HERE I COME.

DID YOU KNOW YOU CAN DIAL 3-1-1 AND GET INFORMATION?
ABOUT WHAT?

ALL SORTS OF STUFF. YOU CAN ASK QUESTIONS ABOUT CITY SERVICES, STRAY ANIMALS, BUILDING PERMITS, UTILITIES, PARKS, POTHOLES, YOU NAME IT.

Beep Boop Boop
12/4
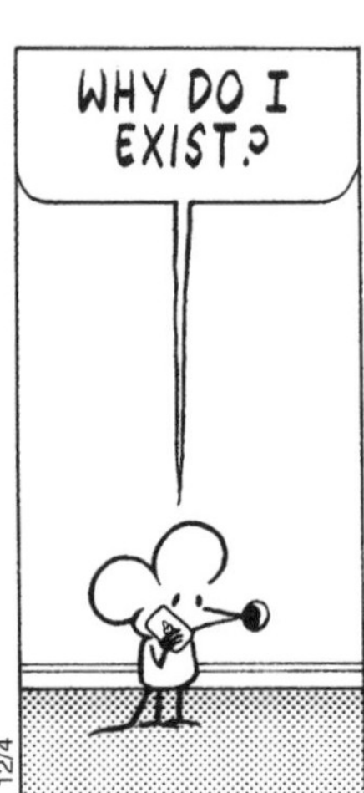
WHY DO I EXIST?

THEY WERE NO HELP.

DID YOU SEE THAT GUY IN THE PAPER WHO WISHES ITALY COULD RETURN TO THE DAYS OF THE DICTATOR BENITO MUSSOLINI?
HE'S IN FAVOR OF THE MAN THEY CALLED 'IL DUCE'?

YEAH, AND TO RAISE MONEY, HE'S GROWING HIS OWN FRUITS AND VEGETABLES.
WHAT'S THE NAME OF THE BUSINESS?
12/5

'PRO-DUCE PRODUCED PRODUCE.'

I'M ANTI-YOU.

HEY THERE, GOAT. WELCOME TO MY NEW MUSEUM.
WHAT'S IN IT?
STEP AROUND THESE BOXES AND I'LL SHOW YOU.
WHAT IS IT?
A SCULPTURE OF A BIRD'S HEAD.
12/6

AND THIS?
A TURTLE EATING LETTUCE.
A WOLF HOWLING?
YUP.
WHAT'S THIS ONE?
A SQUARE-HEADED DOG BEGGING FOR FOOD.
AND THAT?
A MORAY EEL RISING OUT OF HIS CAVE TO EAT.
12/6

WELL, THANK YOU, PIG... IT WAS NICE SEEING—
Museum of U.S. States
YOU THINK YOU'RE SO CLEVER.
NINE STATES. NAME 'EM ALL.
I ONLY SEE A BIRD'S HEAD.

PARDON ME, SIR, BUT YOUR NUMBER IS UP.
12/7

OHHH, GAWWWD!! I'M TOO YOUNG!! I HAVE A WIFE!! AND KIDS!! OHH GAWWWD!!!

MAYBE NEXT TIME I'LL COME TO THE DELI ALONE.
YOU GONNA GET YOUR SANDWICH OR NOT, PAL?
NOW SERVING
61

MAKE ME FEEL BETTER, PIG. MY EX-WIFE IS DATING ONE CLOWN AFTER ANOTHER.
AW, STEPH. THAT'S PROBABLY NOT A NICE THING TO SAY.

THANK YOU, RONALD... I HAD A WONDERFUL NIGHT.
12/8

SHE'S A SUCKER FOR A HAPPY MEAL.

DID YOU KNOW THAT FOUR BABIES ARE BORN EVERY SECOND?
WHERE'D YOU READ THAT?
12/9

BOOM. OUT POP EIGHT BABIES.
WHAT?

BOOM. OUT POP FOUR MORE.
AH. I SEE WHAT YOU'RE DOING. SO I'M GONNA TAKE A COUPLE MINUTES TO USE THE RESTROOM AND WHEN I COME BACK, MAYBE YOU'LL BE DONE.

AND THERE'LL BE 480 NEW BABIES!!
WILL THEY BE COMMUTING ON MY FREEWAY?

HI, PIG... I'D LIKE YOU TO MEET MY FRIEND, BRIAN.... HE DESIGNS THE AUTOCORRECT FEATURE FOR ALL THE TEXTS PEOPLE SEND.
12/10

THAT SEEMS SO COMPLEX. HOW DO YOU KNOW WHAT WORD TO CHANGE IT TO?
I FIND THE MOST EMBARRASSING AND PICK THAT.

THAT SEEMS UNFAIR.
PROGRAMMERS NEED JOY IN THEIR LIVES, ALSO!

DO YOU FORGIVE AND FORGET THE BAD THINGS PEOPLE DO TO YOU?
YES. I FORGIVE PEOPLE ALL THE TIME.

BUT I NEVER FORGET DIDDLY!!
12/11

NEVER MIND.
REMEMBERING IS THE FIRST STEP TO EXACTING VENGEANCE.

WITH ALL THE OVERPOPULATION IN THE WORLD, WHAT IF WE MADE A RULE THAT COUPLES CAN HAVE NO MORE THAN TWO CHILDREN?
WHY TWO?

BECAUSE THAT ALLOWS THE COUPLE TO REPLICATE ONLY THEMSELVES. AND BESIDES, NO FAMILY'S THIRD CHILD HAS EVER CONTRIBUTED ANYTHING WORTHWHILE TO THIS WORLD.
12/12

I KNOW YOU KNOW I'M A THIRD CHILD.
I REITERATE MY POSITION.
GEE, MAYBE TWO *SHOULD* BE THE RULE.

RAT
TO: MY FAMILY
RULES FOR THIS YEAR'S CHRISTMAS VISIT:

NO JUDGING ME. THAT INCLUDES MY CLOTHES, WEIGHT, CAR, AND WHO I'M DATING.

NO DISCUSSING POLITICS. YOU ARE ALL LOONS.

I do not find your baby/small child as endearing as you do. Please keep this in mind when they are screaming or throwing objects at my head.

Please don't tell me how to live my life. Remember, I see you as loons.

And please do not brag about your own life. It makes me want to shove your head into the rear end of the turkey.

Lastly, none of these rules apply to me.
I AM GREAT.

12/13

COMMUNICATION IS THE KEY TO A HAPPY FAMILY.

YAP YAP YAP YAP YAP YAP YAP YAP
GEEZ, SON, YOU NEVER STOP TALKING AND ASKING QUESTIONS. HOW 'BOUT BEING QUIET NOW AND THEN?

One day, he go away to school and he never answer any of you texts and all you dreams come true.
12/14

YAP YAP YAP YAP YAP YAP YAP YAP

HEY, RAT. HOW'S EVERYTHING GOING?
GREAT. NO PROBLEMS AT ALL.
12/15

OHHH?
WHO THE G☆#@ ARE YOU?
THE JINXIES. YOU BRAGGED ABOUT HAVING NO PROBLEMS, SO WE'RE HERE TO G☆#@ UP YOUR ENTIRE LIFE.

KNOCK ON WOOD! KNOCK ON WOOD! KNOCK ON WOOD!
TOO LATE.
SPEAKING OF WOOD, YOUR HOUSE BURNS DOWN THIS WEEK.

WHY ARE YOU ALL DRESSED UP, NEIGHBOR NANCY?
I'M MEETING A GUY I MET ONLINE. BUT I'M A LITTLE WORRIED HE WON'T LIKE ME IN PERSON. I HAVE SUCH A SQUEAKY VOICE.

FSSHHHH
12/16

WD-40 DOESN'T WORK FOR THAT.

HEY, HOLLY! I NEVER HEARD FROM YOU AFTER OUR DATE LAST WEEK.
YEAH... I'M SORRY ABOUT THAT. I JUST FELT LIKE YOU WERE A LITTLE TOO CLINGY.

CLINGY? ME?
WHAT'S THAT ON YOUR CHEST?

A TATTOO OF YOUR FACE.
12/17

WOMEN ARE SO HARD TO FIGURE OUT.

WHAT ARE ALL YOU GUYS DOING?
WE'VE BEEN CAMPING OUT FOR TODAY'S OPENING OF 'STAR WARS, EPISODE SEVEN.'

12/18
THE MOVIE WILL STILL BE HERE TOMORROW.

NERDS WITH LIGHTSABERS ARE A DANGEROUS BUNCH.

YO, ZEBRA.... HOW YOU DOING?

I'M FINE, BUT MY COUSIN'S NOT VERY HAPPY AT ALL.
WHAT'S EATING HIM?
12/19

A LION.

USUALLY, THAT'S NOT SO LITERAL.

Thank you for downloading our new smartphone app.

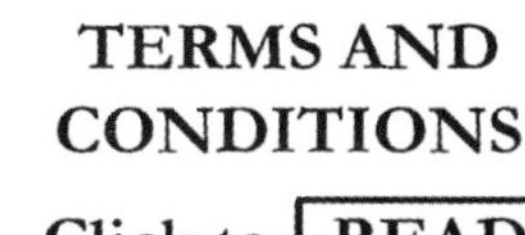

TERMS AND CONDITIONS

Click to READ

Click to ACCEPT

Wow, okay. You're the first guy who didn't just click ACCEPT. But okay, here goes.

TERMS AND CONDITIONS

You have no rights.

We will violate your privacy.

We will track your every movement.

We will sell all of this information to anyone who wants it.

12/20

If we find anything really embarrassing, we will pass it around the office and laugh.

All of the above may accidentally be exposed to the entire world.

If so, oopsy-doopsies.

P.S. You are hosed.

ARE YOU GONNA SPEND THE HOLIDAYS WITH YOUR LOVED ONES?
LOVED ONES?

RELATIVES.
YOU SAID 'LOVED ONES.'

'LOVED ONES' MEANS RELATIVES.
WHAT?
12/21

SOME PEOPLE LOVE THEIR RELATIVES.
WOULD THEY LIKE TO TRADE RELATIVES?

HAVE YOU EVER NOTICED HOW EVERYONE'S CHRISTMAS CARD IS NOW A PHOTO OF THEIR FAMILY ON SOME EXOTIC VACATION, AS IF TO SAY, 'MY FAMILY DID THIS THIS YEAR AND YOURS DID NOT'?
12/22

SO?
SO I DID ONE OF THOSE CARDS MYSELF THIS YEAR. HERE, HAVE A LOOK.

Merry Christmas from my #$%&$#& backyard

COMPETE WITH THAT, SAFARI-TAKING YUPPIES!
MOW YOUR LAWN.

HEY, GOAT... I'D LIKE TO INTRODUCE YOU TO NEGATIVE NICK. HE'S RATHER NEGATIVE.
HOW NEGATIVE?
12/23

WHOOOOSH

DID HE JUST SUCK ALL THE LIGHT OUT OF THE ROOM?
IT HAPPENS.

MERRY CHRISTMAS, RAT! HERE'S YOUR GIFT.
THANKS.

GEE, NOT TO MAKE THIS AWKWARD, BUT I THOUGHT YOU SAID THIS WAS A GIFT *EXCHANGE*.
IT IS.

I GO TO THE STORE AND EXCHANGE YOUR GIFT FOR SOMETHING BETTER.

YOU WOULDN'T.
WELL, NOT IF YOU BOUGHT BETTER GIFTS.
12/24

THERE ARE TOO MANY PEOPLE IN THE WORLD AND NOT ENOUGH SPACE FOR US ALL, SO I'VE FIGURED OUT A SOLUTION—GOING UP.
BUILDING MORE MULTI-STORY HOUSING?

PUTTING SMALL PEOPLE ON THE BACKS OF BIG PEOPLE.
HONEY, I'LL BE LATE FOR DINNER TONIGHT. FRED'S WALKING SLOW.
12/25

I SEE ISSUES WITH THAT.
WELL, OF COURSE HE'S GONNA EAT WITH US. I LIVE ON HIM NOW.

I'M WORRIED ABOUT MY HAMSTER LATELY. ALL HE DOES IS SPEND HIS ENTIRE DAY ENCASED IN HIS HAMSTER BALL.
ISN'T THAT JUST HOW THEY HAVE FUN?

I'M AVOIDING EBOLA.
12/26

THESE ARE DARK TIMES.
NOBODY SNEEZE.

Meh.

The composition is jejune at best.

And is it neo-Marxist or a self-conscious parody of neo-Marxism?

I'd say it fails on both counts.

At best, I'd say we're looking at postmodern blather.

Neither avant-garde nor revelatory in its scope.

12/27

YOU SHOULD NOT BE WRITING A GUIDE TO PARENTING.
BUT LITTLE KIDS NEED GUIDANCE.
HEY, KID, DON'T QUIT YOUR DAY JOB!

I'M TRAINING FOR A MARATHON, PIG, AND I NEED YOU TO KEEP TRACK OF MY TIMES ON THIS SHEET. BUT THERE'S NOT MUCH SPACE, SO ABBREVIATE.
12/28

SURE. DO YOU WANT 'HRS' FOR HOURS?
YES. AND DO AN ABBREVIATION FOR SECONDS ALSO.

OKAY. DO YOU WANT 'SECS'?

RUNNERS HAVE VERY SHORT TEMPERS.

DUDE... WHAT'S THAT ON YOUR HEAD?
IT'S CALLED A TOP KNOT, YOU MORON. AND IT'S VERY HIP.
12/29

SNIP

SOMETIMES YOU JUST HAVE TO SAVE PEOPLE FROM THEMSELVES.

HEY, WAS THAT YOU WHO JUST DROVE BY ME IN A GRAY HONDA ACCORD?
YEAH. BUT I SLOWED DOWN AND GAVE YOU THE RIGHT OF WAY.
12/30

YOU DIDN'T BOW.

CYCLISTS ARE FASCISTS IN TIGHT PANTS.

YOU KNOW THAT CUTE FAMILY PORTRAIT SOME PEOPLE TAKE NOWADAYS WHERE EACH OF THEM DRESSES UP IN MATCHING CLOTHES?
YEAH, WHY?

IT MAKES ME SICK.
12/31

I HATE WHEN I AGREE WITH YOU.
CONGRESS, DO SOMETHING!

HEY, PIG... ANY NEW YEAR'S RESOLUTIONS THIS YEAR?

JUST THIS NEW 'EAT WHAT YOU WANT' DIET.
HOW DOES IT WORK?

YOU GET FAT.
1/1

SOUNDS LIKE YOU DON'T KNOW A LOT ABOUT NUTRITION.

WHAT CAN I GET YOU TO DRINK?
DO YOU HAVE WARM BEAVERS GETTING OLDER?
MENU
1/2

WHAT'S THAT?
I DUNNO. BUT RIGHT HERE YOU OFFER A WARM BEAVER THAT AGES.
MENU

'WARM BEVERAGES.'
MENU

THAT DOESN'T SOUND NEARLY AS INTERESTING.

HALL OF
STATE
MOTTOS

WYOMING

Equal
rights.

OHIO

With God,
all things are
possible!

TEXAS

Friendship

RHODE ISLAND

HOPE!

NEW HAMPSHIRE

LIVE FREE
OR
DIE!!!

NEVER END
YOUR STATE
MOTTO TOUR
WITH NEW
HAMPSHIRE.
THEY'RE
A
SCARY
PEOPLE.

WHAT ARE YOU READING, GOAT?
THIS BOOK ON THE ASSASSINATION OF GARFIELD.

ALL THE LASAGNA HE'LL NEVER EAT!!!

JAMES GARFIELD. PRESIDENT.
OH. WHO CARES ABOUT HIM?

HAVE YOU EVER HEARD OF 'HELICOPTER' PARENTS?
NO. WHAT ARE THEY?

THEY'RE THESE PARENTS NOWADAYS WHO HOVER CONSTANTLY OVER THEIR CHILDREN AND SWOOP IN QUICKLY WHENEVER THERE'S A PROBLEM.

MY PARENTS WERE MORE LIKE A DERAILED TRAIN.

I SEE.
BUT THE CRASHES WERE SPECTACULAR.

REMEMBER THE STORY ABOUT THAT RIP VAN WINKLE GUY WHO FALLS ASLEEP AND WAKES UP IN THE FUTURE?
YEAH. WHY?

BECAUSE IT JUST HAPPENED TO ME.
WHAT ARE YOU TALKING ABOUT?

I WENT TO SLEEP AND WHEN I WOKE UP, IT WAS TWENTY MINUTES LATER!

HIS BRAIN SHOULD BE STUDIED.

And dat when mom ees grow tiny leetle paws, like hamster paws.
REALLY?

Reely. So small dey call dem 'mini' paws. And dat how it get its name.
1/7

THAT IS NOT WHAT MENOPAUSE IS.
HELP.
Tomorrow me teach you 'bout hot flushes.

I THINK I JUST DID THE BEST WRITING OF MY LIFE.
GOOD FOR YOU, GOAT. POST IT ON THE INTERNET FOR ALL THE NICE PEOPLE TO SEE.

GOOD IDEA.
CLICK

MEH
Embarrassing
TRY MUCH?
#%&#$ you, poser.
YOU SUCK, BRO
%#& @$# $#%
DON'T QUIT YOUR DAY JOB!!!!!!!!!
What crap.
1/8

I'VE MET NICER PEOPLE IN A PRISON RIOT.
OH, YEAH. PRISON'S MUCH FRIENDLIER.

I'VE DETERMINED THAT THE INTERNET IS BESIEGED BY PEOPLE WHO JUST WANT TO VENT ANONYMOUSLY.
SO?

SO TO MAKE THE INTERNET A KINDER PLACE, I'VE DECIDED TO GIVE THOSE PEOPLE AN ALTERNATIVE VENUE.

'MAD MEN' SUCKS AFTER SEASON FIVE!!
The BOX O' ANONYMOUS VENTING
1/9

NOT AS SATISFYING.
SHOUT LOUDER.

PIG WENT ON A DATE WITH THAT NEW GIRL LAST NIGHT.
WAS IT THE ONE HE WAS TRYING TO IMPRESS?

YEAH. HE WANTED TO SHOW HER HOW SOPHISTICATED HE WAS, SO HE BRAGGED ABOUT ALL HIS TRAVELS.
DID THAT IMPRESS HER?

NO, BECAUSE THEN SHE ASKED HIM IF HE TRAVELLED OUTSIDE THE CONTINENT AND HE DIDN'T KNOW IF HE LIVED IN NORTH AMERICA OR NOT.
SO WHAT'D SHE SAY?

SHE EXPLAINED HOW YOU KNOW WHETHER YOU LIVE OUT OF THE CONTINENT OR IN IT.
AND WHAT'D HE SAY?
1/10

I'M IN CONTINENT!!

SHE MUST HAVE BEEN SO IMPRESSED.
SHE DID BUY HIM DIAPERS.

COME TO OUR DEALERSHIP AND CHECK OUT OUR TERRIFIC SELECTION OF PRE-OWNED VEHICLES.

IT'S CALLED A USED CAR!!
1/11

I CAN'T TAKE IT ANYMORE.
THE SANITATION ENGINEER IS AT THE DOOR. HE SAYS YOU CALLED HIM A GARBAGEMAN.

PIG REALLY HAS A CHIP ON HIS SHOULDER.
WHAT KIND OF CHIP?

COW CHIP. I FELL ASLEEP IN THE PASTURE.

YOU JUST KEEP GETTING CLASSIER.
1/12

I SAT IN TRAFFIC FOR TWO HOURS THIS AFTERNOON. AS I DO EVERY DAY.
SO?

SO I HAVE A MESSAGE FOR ALL THE GOOD PEOPLE OF THE WORLD.
WHAT'S THAT?
1/13

COOL IT WITH THE BABIES!!!

FEEL BETTER?
SCREAMING IS THE NEXT BEST THING TO SOLVING PROBLEMS.

HEY, CRASH TEST GUY. HOW'S WORK?
GOOD. BEEN MAKING A LOT OF PROGRESS LATELY. REALLY LEARNING THE JOB.

TERRIFIC. DO YOU THINK YOUR PROGRESS WILL CONTINUE?
NO. AT SOME POINT I'LL HIT A WALL.
1/14

THEY SHOULD USE YOU INSTEAD.

LET'S CHANGE THE CHANNEL. I DON'T LIKE THIS SHOW.
I CAN'T FIND THE REMOTE.

OH, GOD. WHAT DO WE DO?
I KNOW.
1/15

THAT IS NOT AN EMERGENCY.
911 OPERATOR

IF YOU COULD ELIMINATE ONE MALADY FROM THE FACE OF THE EARTH, WHAT WOULD IT BE?

UNDERWEAR LABELS. THEY ANNOY THE @☆#@ OUT OF ME.
1/16

PERHAPS THINK MORE BROADLY.
FINE. SHIRT LABELS TOO.

WHAT ARE YOU DOING, GOAT?
A LITTLE THOUGHT EXERCISE.

YOU WRITE DOWN EACH OF THE THINGS THAT ARE IMPORTANT IN YOUR LIFE ON THESE LITTLE CARDS. THEN YOU ELIMINATE ONE CARD AT A TIME UNTIL YOU GET TO THE ONE THING THAT'S MOST IMPORTANT TO YOU.

WHAT'S YOURS?

LOVE

WOW. THAT'S BEAUTIFUL.
YEAH... HERE, TAKE SOME CARDS AND TRY IT YOURSELF.

1/17

CHEESE

THIS IS WHY WE DON'T HAVE THESE DISCUSSIONS.
CHEESE CONQUERS ALL.

WHAT ARE YOU READING, RAT?
THIS STORY ON A LAW THAT THE STATE OF MISSOURI MAY OR MAY NOT PASS.

WHAT'S HOLDING THEM UP?
THEY ONLY WANT TO PASS IT IF OTHER STATES JOIN THEM IN PASSING SIMILAR LAWS AT THE SAME TIME.
1/18

MISSOURI LOVES COMPANY.

NO ONE WANTS YOUR COMPANY.

IF THERE IS ANYTHING WE CAN DO TO MAKE YOUR FLIGHT MORE COMFORTABLE, PLEASE JUST LET US KNOW.

PLEASE PUT ALL THE BABIES IN A SOUNDPROOF BOX.
1/19

THEY NEVER MEAN IT.

STEPHAN, YOUR DRIVER'S LICENSE RENEWAL FORM CAME IN THE MAIL. I FILLED IT OUT AND MADE YOU AN ORGAN DONOR.
WHAT FOR?

BECAUSE I'M GIVING YOU AWAY, PIECE BY PIECE.
1/20

OUR MARRIAGE COULD BE HEALTHIER.
IF YOU'RE LUCKY, I'LL WAIT 'TIL YOU DIE.

WHAT ARE YOU DOING, PIG?
THROWING AWAY OUR WATERMELONS. THEY WEIGH TOO MUCH.

WHAT ARE YOU TALKING ABOUT?
I'VE CONCLUDED THAT THE REASON I WEIGH SO MUCH IS THAT I EAT FOOD THAT WEIGHS A LOT. SO FROM NOW ON, I'M ONLY GONNA EAT FOOD THAT IS LIGHT.
1/21

CHIPS, DONUTS, AND COTTON CANDY.
I'LL BE RAIL THIN IN NO TIME.

WHAT DO YOU HAVE THERE, RAT?
IT'S THE NEW SMARTPHONE 6. IT JUST CAME OUT TODAY AND IT'S LIGHT YEARS AHEAD OF THE 5.
SALE ON
RTPHONES
1/22

SMARTPHONE
7
OUT TOMORRO
ALL NEW FEATURES!
FASTE BIGGE

TECH COMPANIES ARE EVIL.
SALE ON
RTPHONES

WHAT ARE YOU DOING, RAT?
LYING ON MY BACK WITH A BEER.

WHAT FOR?
BECAUSE IN THOUSANDS OF YEARS, NOTHING WE'VE ACCOMPLISHED WILL BE REMEMBERED, SO YOU CAN KILL YOURSELF TRYING TO ACHIEVE THINGS, OR YOU CAN DO THIS.
1/23

THOSE POOR ACHIEVERS.

Danny Donkey's girlfriend was angry.

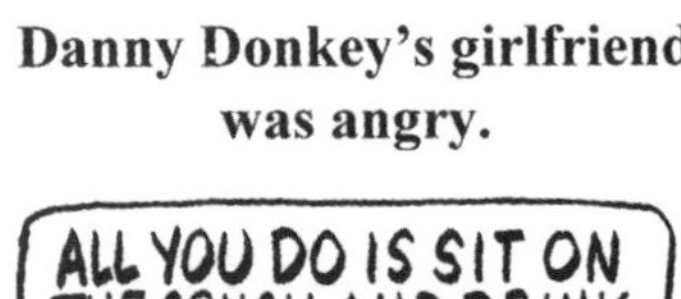

ALL YOU DO IS SIT ON THE COUCH AND DRINK BEER.

So she gave him an ultimatum.

YOU NEED TO FIND YOUR PASSION IN LIFE AND PURSUE IT, OR I'M LEAVING YOU.

"Here," she said, handing him an envelope. "Write down your passion and slip it in here, and in six weeks we'll open the envelope and see if you've taken any concrete steps towards achieving your passion."

So Danny Donkey did what she asked.

But then did nothing.

When the six weeks were up, Danny's girlfriend confronted him.

OH, DANNY...YOU DID NOTHING TO PURSUE YOUR PASSION... THAT'S SO AWFUL...WHAT WAS IT, ANYWAYS?

1/24

Sit on the couch and drink beer.

Danny's girlfriend left him anyways.

BUT HE PURSUED HIS PASSION!
LIFE JUST ISN'T FAIR.
BEING LAZY IS NOT A PASSION!

WHAT ARE YOU READING, GOAT?
THIS STORY ABOUT A GUY WHO COMMITTED MATRICIDE. SORRY... DO YOU KNOW WHAT THAT IS?
THE TIMES
1/25

BLAM BLAM

NO.

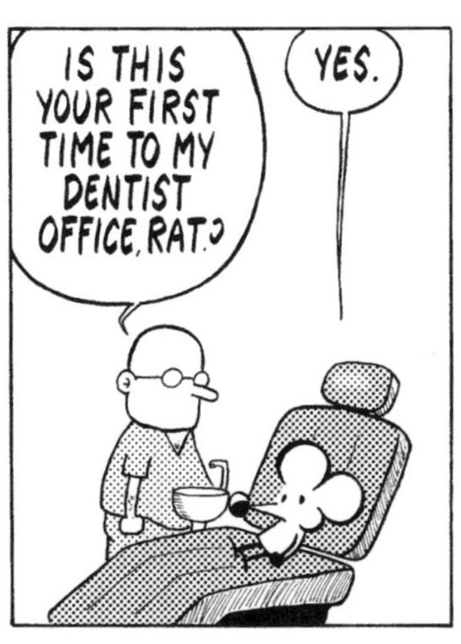
IS THIS YOUR FIRST TIME TO MY DENTIST OFFICE, RAT?
YES.

THEN LET ME TELL YOU HOW THIS IS GONNA WORK.
OKAY.
1/26

MY HYGIENIST WILL CLEAN YOUR TEETH. AFTER THAT, I'LL SWOOP IN AND MAKE YOU FEEL INADEQUATE, LAZY, AND DOOMED.

YOU HAVE TO ADMIRE HIS HONESTY.

HOW DO MY TEETH LOOK?
NOT GOOD. YOU'RE NOT BRUSHING ENOUGH. YOU'RE NOT FLOSSING ENOUGH. YOU'RE NOT COMING INTO THIS OFFICE ENOUGH.
1/27

YOU'RE A SAD DISAPPOINTMENT. A REAL PIECE OF G#☆#. AND WHY YOU'RE ALLOWED TO BREATHE THE SAME AIR AS ME CONFOUNDS MY LARGE EGO AND HAIRY FOREARMS.

MUCH BETTER THAN MY LAST APPOINTMENT.

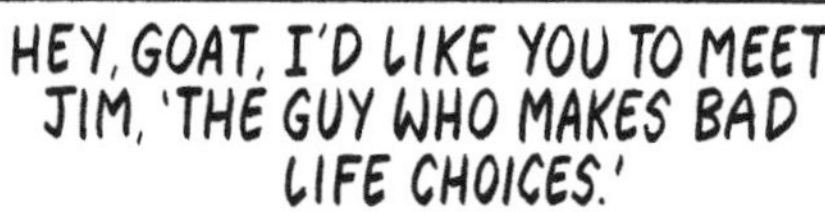

HEY, GOAT, I'D LIKE YOU TO MEET JIM, 'THE GUY WHO MAKES BAD LIFE CHOICES.'

1/28

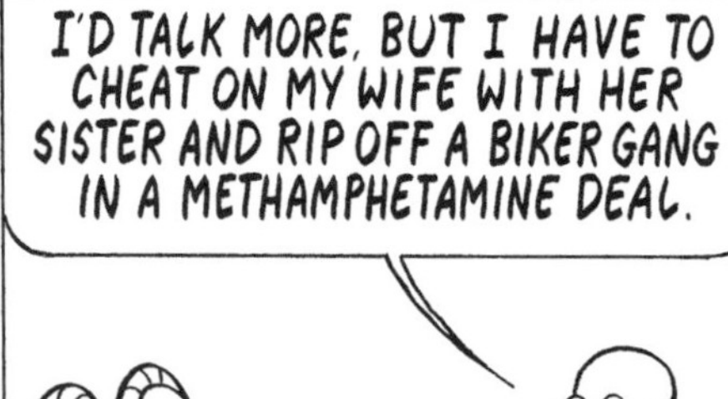

I'D TALK MORE, BUT I HAVE TO CHEAT ON MY WIFE WITH HER SISTER AND RIP OFF A BIKER GANG IN A METHAMPHETAMINE DEAL.

HE'LL BE A SHORT TERM CHARACTER.

WHERE WERE YOU TODAY, RAT?
SHOPPING. I GOT A LAZY SUSAN TO PUT ON OUR KITCHEN TABLE.

I'M NOT DOING A @#@☆#¶@ THING.
1/29

SUSAN HAS A VERY BAD ATTITUDE.

HEY, RAT. WELCOME TO MY COCKTAIL PARTY. CAN I GET YOU A BEVERAGE?
DUDE... TALK LIKE A NORMAL PERSON.

WHAT DO YOU MEAN?
YOU DON'T HAVE TO SAY 'BEVERAGE.' JUST SAY 'DRINK' AND STOP BEING A HOITY TOITY FATFACE.

1/30

CAN I GET YOU A LIBATION?
CURSE YOUR SNOOTY FATFACE!

HEY, STEPH, WHEN YOU LIVED IN THE DORMS IN COLLEGE, DID IT BUG YOU WHEN YOUR ROOMMATE TALKED ALL THE TIME ON HIS CELL PHONE?

HE DIDN'T HAVE ONE.
WHY NOT?

THEY DIDN'T EXIST.
DIDN'T EXIST? WELL, WHAT ABOUT WHEN HE SKYPED SOMEONE ON HIS LAPTOP?

NO LAPTOPS.
WHAT DO YOU MEAN NO LAPTOPS? THEN HOW DID YOU SKYPE PEOPLE?

NO SKYPE.
HOW COULD YOU HAVE NO SKYPE?

NO INTERNET FOR IT TO RUN ON.
1/31

DUDE, HOW OLD *ARE* YOU?
TECHNOLOGY MOVED FAST!
NEED SOME WHALE OIL FOR YOUR LAMPS, STEPH?
WHALE OIL

Whuh for dinner, woomun?
Well, Larry, since you're unable to catch a zebra, we're having tofu.

TOFU?! Dat huge insult to Larry manhood.
EAT YOUR TOFU, LARRY. IT'S NOT LIKE ANYONE IS GONNA SEE YOU.

2/1

Me turn in man card right now.
Hang on. Me take photo for Eenstagram.

WHAT ARE YOU DOING, RAT?
WAITING FOR PUNXSUTAWNEY PHIL... IF HE COMES OUT OF HIS HOLE AND SEES HIS SHADOW, THERE ARE SIX MORE WEEKS OF WINTER. BUT IF HE COMES OUT AND SEES NO SHADOW, IT WILL BE AN EARLY SPRING.

AAAHHHHHH
2/2

THAT DOESN'T BODE WELL.

Hey, Larry, word ees you get caught eating tofu.
Yeah. Dey ees call you 'Tofu Larry.'
Stoopid wife serve. But me no eat. Look, she put note in Larry lunch to apoleegize.

DEAR LARRY, ENJOY YOUR VEGGIE BURGER!
2/3

Dis look bad, Larry.
Hey, look. Bag fit on head.

OKAY, woomun.. First you serve Larry TOFU. Den VEGGIE BURGER. Ees you TRYING lose Larry man card forever?!
FINE. SO TELL ME, LARRY, WHAT EXACTLY IS AN ACCEPTABLE MEAL FOR YOUR STUPID MAN CARD?

Well, you know how at end of movies, it say, 'No aneemals was harmed in making of dis film'?
YEAH.

HARM SOME ANEEMALS!
HERE...DO ANIMAL CRACKERS COUNT?
2/4

WHAT ARE YOU DOING, ZEBRA?
I'M DESIGNING A LONG BOW WITH A UNIQUE SHAPE. I'M EVEN GETTING CELEBRITY ATHLETES TO PUT THEIR NAME ON IT.

LIKE WHO?
FORMER N.F.L. STARS BO JACKSON AND HOWIE LONG. THEY ALL LIKE ITS UNIQUE OBLONG SHAPE. NOW I JUST NEED A NAME FOR IT.
2/5

THE BO LONG OBLONG LONG BOW?

KEEP ME OUT OF THESE.

ARE YOU RELIGIOUS?
WHEN IT'S CONVENIENT.

WHAT DOES THAT MEAN?
WHEN I WANT TO JUDGE OTHERS OR FEAR IMPENDING DEATH.
2/6

I THINK THAT'S CALLED OPPORTUNISM.
THEN I'M ITS PATRON SAINT!

EXCUSE ME, SIR. WHY IS WENDY'S CLOSED? I NEED MY FAVORITE BURGER.
WE LOST OUR BEST SECURITY GUARD, FRED.
WENDY'S
CLOSED

SO?
SO UNTIL WE FIND ANOTHER GUY AS GOOD AS FRED, WE JUST CAN'T RE-OPEN.
WENDY'S
CLOSED

BUT WHAT'S SO VALUABLE THAT YOU NEED A SECURITY GUARD?
WELL, IF YOU MUST KNOW, WE HAVE SOME VERY VALUABLE REAMS OF PAPER.
WENDY'S
CLOSED

FOR WHAT?
TO KEEP TRACK OF OUR NUCLEAR FISSION EXPER-IMENTS. WE DO THAT HERE, TOO.
WENDY'S
CLOSED

SO WHAT DOES ALL THAT MEAN?
IT MEANS NO BURGERS FOR YOU. UNLESS YOU WANT TO BE SECURITY GUARD.

WENDY'S, LET ME IN, I WANT TO BE YOUR FRED, I WANT TO GUARD YOUR REAMS AND FISSIONS!

2/7

BABY, I WAS BORN TO PUN.

CAN I HELP YOU?
YEAH. YOU'RE MISTER BROWN. YOU TAUGHT ME ALGEBRA IN HIGH SCHOOL.
2/8

SO?
SO I HAVE SOME ALGEBRA FOR YOU.

IN THE 7,649 DAYS THAT HAVE PASSED SINCE HIGH SCHOOL, I HAVE NOT USED ALGEBRA ONE G&#G$#G TIME.

THAT WASN'T REALLY ALGEBRA.
IT WAS STILL CATHARTIC.

WHAT ARE YOU LOOK-ING AT, GOAT?
A TARDIGRADE. THEY'RE MICRO-ANIMALS THAT CAN SURVIVE AND ADAPT TO ANYTHING—ABSOLUTE ZERO TEMPERATURES, BOILING TEMPERATURES, EXTREMELY HIGH PRESSURE, MASSIVE AMOUNTS OF RADIATION.

SMOOSH
2/9

AND YET HE STRUGGLES TO FIGURE OUT THE SHOE.

DID YOU LOCK YOUR CAR?
YEAH... SEE, IF I PRESS THE LOCK BUTTON A SECOND TIME, IT HONKS TO TELL ME IT'S LOCKED.
CLICK
HONK

WHAT HAPPENS IF YOU PRESS IT A THIRD TIME?
CLICK

CHILL, YOU ANAL-RETENTIVE WEIRDO
2/10

A FOURTH TIME COULD BE INTERESTING.

WHAT ARE YOU DOING, DAD?
Mom want re-new wedding vows. So me writing what me gonna say.

THAT'S WONDERFUL, DAD. LET'S HEAR IT.
"Me, Larry, ees take wife to have and to hold..."

"For better or worse, or much worse, which ees how it usually ees."

UH... DAD.
"But being meeserable ees okay, because one day me die."
2/11

HOW DO YOU KNOW IF YOU'RE A NARCISSIST?
IF AT LEAST FIFTY PERCENT OF YOUR PHOTOS ON FACEBOOK ARE OF YOUR OWN FACE.

WHAT IF IT'S A HUNDRED PERCENT?

TELL ME YOU'RE KIDDING.
OH, WAIT... THERE'S SOME LOSER IN THE BACKGROUND HERE.
2/12

THIS STRIP GIVES US A PLATFORM TO ADVOCATE. SO I SAY WE ADVOCATE.

FOR WHAT?
ELIMINATING V.D.

V.D.?
VALENTINE'S DAY. IT'S A STUPID HOLIDAY AND NOBODY LIKES IT.

NEXT TIME JUST SAY 'VALENTINE'S DAY.'
TOO LATE. I'VE MADE SIGNS.
V.D.
2/13

GOVERNMENT 101
by Rat
Please take notes.
Hello, Senator. Here's a million dollars for your Super Pac. I'd like you to kill a banking bill that's hurting my business.
Whoa, whoa. You've stated a quid pro quo. And that makes this ILLEGAL.

A quid pro what?
Quid pro quo. An explicit exchange of money for a favor. And that is illegal, immoral, and repulsive.

So now what?
So go back out. Then come back in. And this time just say you'd like to donate a million dollars to my Super Pac.

Hello. I'd like to donate a million dollars to your Super Pac.
Well, thank you, sir. How is business?

Not good. There's a banking bill I don't like.
I don't like that bill either. I think I'll kill it.

And what was that?
LEGAL!

2/14
I THINK OUR SYSTEM NEEDS FIXING.
HOW MUCH MORE FIXED CAN IT GET?
YAY! THE SYSTEM IS FIXED! THE SYSTEM IS FIXED!

I DON'T MIND AMERICANS NOT BEING INFORMED.

BUT IS IT SO HARD TO REMEMBER THAT IF YOU LIKE TO DRIVE AT A RESPONSIBLE SPEED...

STAY OUT OF THE G#G☆#G# LEFT LANE!!
2/15

THIS HAS BEEN A PUBLIC SERVICE ANNOUNCEMENT.

WHAT THE HECK HAPPENED HERE?
I THOUGHT IT'D BE FUN TO BUILD A DAM ACROSS THE CREEK IN OUR BACKYARD, BUT NOW I'VE FLOODED EVERYTHING

WHAT DO YOU KNOW ABOUT BUILDING DAMS?
NOTHING.
2/16

YOU DAM FOOL!

YOU ANGER ME TO NO END.
THIS STUPID DAM THING.
COMIC STRIP CENSOR

HELLO?
HEY, GOAT... IT'S ME, RAT. I'M JUST CALLING TO WISH YOU A VERY HAPPY BIRTHDAY.

IT'S NOT MY BIRTHDAY. MY BIRTHDAY'S NOT FOR ANOTHER SIX MONTHS.

YEAH, I KNOW. BUT YOU'RE NOT THAT IMPORTANT TO ME, SO THE ODDS ARE I'LL FORGET ON THE ACTUAL DAY.
2/17

THAT WAS ALMOST CONSIDERATE.

GOOD MORNING, SIR. HAVE YOU MET MY L'IL SCOUTS TROOP?
I SURE HAVEN'T. WHAT'S THAT LITTLE MERIT BADGE ON THEIR VEST FOR?

FIGHTING WITH CHAINS.
2/18

MAYBE THEY SHOULD WORK ON BUILDING CAMPFIRES INSTEAD.
OH, WE CAN BUILD FIRES.
GASOLINE

HOW COME YOU NEVER PLANT ANY COLORFUL FLOWERS IN YOUR BACKYARD, PIG?
BECAUSE THE DEER EAT THEM.

THE DEER EAT EVERYTHING?

IS THIS ALL YOU HAVE IN THE FRIDGE?
2/19

EVERYTHING.

WHAT'S THAT?
NEW WATCH. I JUST BOUGHT IT.

YOU JUST GOT A FANCY WATCH TO SHOW OFF.
NO, I DIDN'T. I GOT IT BECAUSE IT'S A GOOD WATCH AND IT TELLS TIME WELL.

2/20

WANT TO KNOW WHAT TIME IT IS?

TECH SUPPORT. HOW CAN I HELP YOU?
YEAH, I'VE LOADED YOUR SOFTWARE ONTO MY COMPUTER AND NOW THE COMPUTER ISN'T WORKING AT ALL.
BEER

I'M SORRY TO HEAR THAT. LET'S SEE WHAT I CAN DO.
FINE.
BEER

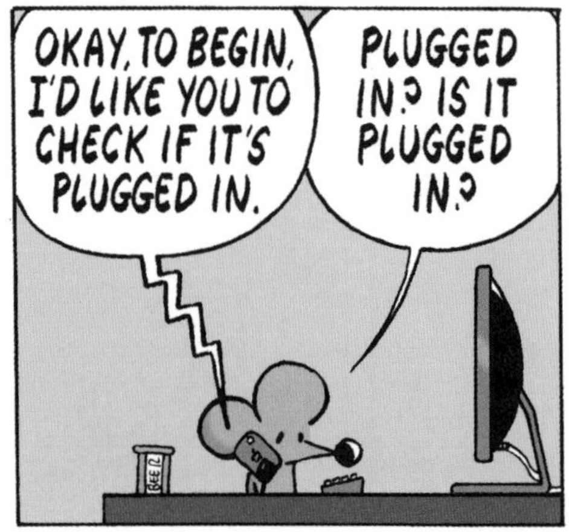
OKAY, TO BEGIN, I'D LIKE YOU TO CHECK IF IT'S PLUGGED IN.
PLUGGED IN? IS IT PLUGGED IN?
BEER

YES, SIR.
I'VE WAITED FORTY MINUTES ON HOLD SO THAT SOME TECH GUY COULD ASK ME *THAT*?
BEER

YES, SIR. IT'S A CHECKLIST I HAVE TO GO THROUGH.
YEAH, WELL HERE'S *MY* CHECKLIST...
BEER

2/21

ITEM 1: STOP BUYING SOFTWARE FROM COMPANIES THAT TREAT ME LIKE A G☆#G☆#☆ MORON! ITEM 2: STOP WASTING FORTY MINUTES ON HOLD TO SPEAK TO SOMEONE AS USELESS AS YOU!

SORRY, SIR, IT'S JUST OUR PROCEDURE THAT I—
CLICK
BEER

HOW LONG HAVE YOU LIVED IN TOWN, NEIGHBOR NANCY?
TWO YEARS. WE MOVED HERE SO MY KIDS COULD BE CLOSER TO THEIR GRANDPARENTS. THEY JUST LOVE HAVING MY KIDS OVER.
2/22

NO, WE DON'T.

PARDON US FOR A MOMENT.
WE DREAD IT, REALLY.
LET US LIVE OUR G☆#G☆#G LIVES!

WHATCHA DOING, NEIGHBOR NANCY?
I WANT TO DROP MY KIDS OFF AT MY FOLKS'. I RANG THE DOORBELL, BUT MAYBE THEY CAN'T HEAR IT.
DID YOU TRY LOOKING IN THE WINDOW?

WE'RE GOING TO HELL FOR THIS.
BETTER THAN BEING WITH THOSE KIDS.
2/23

WHAT ARE YOU DOING, PIG?
I STARTED A WEBSITE TO SELL GOODS TO OLDER PEOPLE. YOU KNOW, LIKE THE CLAPPER, LIFE ALERT, CANES, WALKERS.
2/24

THAT'S A LOT OF ITEMS CRAMMED ONTO THAT ONE WEB PAGE.
YEAH, I KNOW. SO I HAD TO SHORTEN SOME OF THE PRODUCT DESCRIPTIONS.

I DON'T THINK I'D SAY, 'GET THE CLAP.'
YEAH, IT HASN'T SOLD WELL.

HEY, NEIGHBOR NANCY, HOW GOES IT?
NOT WELL. I CAN'T GET MY FOLKS TO EVER TAKE MY KIDS FOR THE DAY.

WHY NOT?
I DON'T KNOW. BUT IT'S RIDICULOUS. I MEAN, WHAT ELSE DO OLD PEOPLE HAVE TO DO ALL DAY? KNIT? SIT IN RECLINERS? WATCH 'JEOPARDY'?

CHUG! CHUG! CHUG!
2/25

MEN
2/26

OUT OF MY WAY, GUYS. I NEED TO USE THE BATHROOM.
THIS ISN'T A BATHROOM. IT'S JUST A ROOM FILLED WITH MEN.

SOME SIGNS ARE SURPRISINGLY LITERAL.

WHAT ARE YOU DOING, RAT?
ELECTRICAL WORK. I'VE TAKEN YOU OFF THE POWER GRID AND PUT YOU ON AN ALTERNATIVE SOURCE OF ENERGY.
2/27

YOU MEAN LIKE SOLAR?
NO. I'VE FIGURED OUT A WAY TO TURN LAUGHTER INTO ENERGY. SO FROM NOW ON, YOUR HOUSE HERE WILL BE POWERED BY ALL THE LAUGHS YOU CREATE WITH YOUR COMIC STRIP.

I'LL PUT YOU BACK ON THE POWER GRID.

I'VE DECIDED TO RUN FOR PRESIDENT.
THAT TAKES BILLIONS OF DOLLARS NOW.

I KNOW. SO I'VE FORMED A SUPER PAC RUN BY DANNY DONKEY AND SNUFFLES THE CAT. IT CAN RAISE UNLIMITED FUNDS FOR ME.
RAT 2016

WELL, NOW WAIT A MINUTE. THE SUPREME COURT SAYS THAT YOU AND THE SUPER PAC CAN'T COORDINATE. IT HAS TO BE TOTALLY INDEPENDENT OF YOU.

OH, I KNOW. SO TO ENSURE THAT, I'VE CONSTRUCTED THIS WALL OF STURDY BEER CANS TO SEPARATE US.

2/28

IT'S NOT FOOLPROOF.

WHAT'S WITH THE HELMET, PIG?
IT'S FOR TIME TRAVEL. THIS HAS BEEN A TOUGH YEAR SO FAR. SO I'M SKIPPING IT AND GOING STRAIGHT TO THE NEXT ONE.

YOU KNOW, THAT'S NOT WHAT 'LEAP YEAR' MEANS.

TOO LATE.
SO LONG, STUPID YEAR!!
2/29

REMEMBER THAT POSTER OF OBAMA THAT JUST SAID 'HOPE'?

YEAH. WHY?
BECAUSE I'VE CREATED A SIMILAR ONE FOR MY 2016 PRESIDENTIAL CAMPAIGN.
3/1

DESPAIR

AT LEAST IT'S HONEST.
AND I KNOW I CAN DELIVER.

NEIGHBOR NANCY CONFRONTS HER KIDS' GRANDPARENTS.
YOU TWO ARE GRANDPARENTS NOW. THAT MEANS THAT IF I WANT TO DROP OFF MY KIDS WITH YOU FOR THE DAY, YOU SHOULD LOOK FORWARD TO IT. I MEAN, WHAT'S BETTER THAN THAT?

EVERYTHING.
3/2

PLEASE TAKE OFF THE HEADPHONES.
YO. WE'RE TUNING YOU OUT.
WORD.

HEY, DAD. CALLED TO SEE IF YOU AND MOM COULD WATCH MY KIDS TODAY. OR ARE YOU TOO BUSY WITH YOUR AGE-INAPPROPRIATE SHENANIGANS?
SORRY. CAN'T DO IT. WE'RE HAVING A PRETTY HOT FOURSOME.

AHHHHHHHHHH

GUESS SHE DOESN'T LIKE BRIDGE.
3/3

OH, WISE ASS ON THE HILL, WHAT IS THE KEY TO LIFE?
LOVE YOUR FELLOW MAN.
WISE ASS ON THE HILL

HOW DOES ONE ACHIEVE THAT?
LIVE HIGH ON A HILL, WHERE YOU DON'T HAVE TO SEE ANY OF THEM.

THAT SEEMS UNFAIR.
WISE ASS ON THE HILL
3/4

OH, WISE ASS ON THE HILL, YOU ONCE SAID THE KEY TO LOVING YOUR FELLOW MAN IS TO LIVE HIGH UP ON A HILL WHERE YOU DON'T HAVE TO SEE ANY OF THEM.
YES, MY SON.

IS THAT STILL TRUE?
YES, MY SON.

YOU'RE RUINING EVERYTHING.
3/5

WHAT ARE YOU DOING, GUARD DUCK?
I VOLUNTEERED TO BE A SCOUTMASTER FOR A TROOP OF L'IL SCOUTS.
COOKIES FOR SALE

WELL, GOOD FOR YOU. LITTLE GIRLS NEED POSITIVE ROLE MODELS. AND YOU'RE SELL-ING COOKIES?
YESSIR. BUT IF YOU CAN EXCUSE ME, WE HAVE A CUSTOMER.
COOKIES FOR SALE

CARE FOR SOME COOKIES, MA'AM?
YOU BET. I'LL TAKE A BOX OF CHOCOLATE CHIP AND A BOX OF PEANUT BUTTER.
COOKIES FOR SALE

WELL, THANK YOU, MA'AM. THAT'S VERY GENEROUS OF YOU.
OH, IT'S MY PLEASURE. I LOVE TO SUPPORT YOUNG GIRLS IN THEIR SCOUTING ENDEAVORS. AND WHAT ARE YOU RAISING MONEY FOR?
3/6

A FLAMETHROWER AND A BOX OF GRENADES.
COOKIES FOR SALE

PERHAPS WE SHOULD BE LESS FORTHCOMING, SALLY.
NO ONE WILL @☆#@ WITH THIS TROOP, MA'AM!
COOKIES FOR SALE

LOOK, GOAT, I GOT NEW LOUVER SHUTTERS.
WHAT'S THAT FUNNY THING STICKING OUT OF THEM?

THAT'S THE LIVER-SHAPED CRANK THAT OPENS THEM. MAKES FOR AN EASY GRIP. DO YOU LIKE IT?
I LOVE IT.
3/7

SO YOU'RE A LIVER LEVER LOUVER LOVER?

NOBODY LOVES YOU.

HEY, NEIGH-BOR PHIL. HOW GOES IT?
GOOD. BEEN EATING NOTHING BUT HEALTHY GRAINS AND NUTS. PLUS, I'VE BEEN GOING FOR LONG HIKES AND TEN-MILE RUNS. IF YOU'RE INTERESTED IN THE LIFESTYLE, I CAN ANSWER ANY QUESTIONS YOU MAY HAVE.

I HAVE A QUESTION.
YES, RAT?
3/8

WHY DO HEALTH-CONSCIOUS PEOPLE LOOK THE LEAST HEALTHY?

HE TOOK HIS GRANOLA AND WENT HOME.
AT LEAST BEER GIVES ME A ROSY GLOW!!

HI MOM. HI DAD. WHERE ARE MY KIDS?
THEY WENT FOR A BIKE RIDE.

WHO'S WATCHING THEM?
WATCHING THEM? WELL, NOT US. WE'RE READING THE PAPER.
3/9

AAHHHHH

PARENTING IS DIFFERENT NOW.

MOM, DAD...WE HAVE TO TALK...WHEN YOU ARE WATCHING MY KIDS, YOU CANNOT LET THEM RIDE THEIR BIKES AROUND THE BLOCK UNSUPERVISED...IT'S IRRESPONSIBLE AND YOU WOULDN'T HAVE DONE THAT WITH ME WHEN I WAS A KID.

WHEN YOU WERE A KID, WE LET YOU FLY BY YOURSELF TO PITTSBURGH.
3/10

HOW AM I EVEN ALIVE?!
THE TRUTH IS WE DIDN'T EVEN KNOW YOU WERE GONE.
OH, WHAT A SUMMER THAT WAS.

HAVE YOU THOUGHT ABOUT WHAT PARTY YOU'RE GONNA BE AFFILIATED WITH IN YOUR RUN FOR PRESIDENT?
NO. WHAT ARE MY OPTIONS?
WELL, ARE YOU A MODERATE SORT OF EISENHOWER REPUBLICAN? A CONSERVATIVE REAGAN REPUBLICAN? A FAR RIGHT DICK CHENEY REPUBLICAN?

WHAT'S ABOUT TWENTY CLICKS TO THE RIGHT OF DICK CHENEY?
3/11

OH, LORD.
YOU'VE HEARD OF COMPASSIONATE CONSERVATISM? MINE WILL BE A COMPASSIONATE TOTALITARIAN DICTATORSHIP.

HEY, PIG...WHY DO YOU HAVE SUCH A THICK WALLET?
I STUFF IT WITH THOSE 'GET OUT OF JAIL FREE' CARDS FROM 'MONOPOLY.'

WHAT FOR?
JUST IN CASE.
3/12

THOSE ONLY WORK IN 'MONOPOLY.'
OH, GREAT. NOW I FEEL LESS SECURE.

3/13

IT SUMMONS A HERD OF BUNNIES THAT PARACHUTE IN AND EAT THE BANK'S C.E.O.

CHOMP CHOMP CHOMP

WHAT ARE ALL THESE LOCKS ON THIS BRIDGE, GOAT?
THEY'RE LOVE LOCKS. COUPLES PUT THEM THERE AS A SYMBOL OF THEIR EVERLASTING, UNBREAKABLE LOVE.

THERE WERE RELATIONSHIP ISSUES.
3/14

WANT TO BUY SOME COOKIES, SIR?
SURE, L'IL SCOUTS. WHAT ARE YOU RAISING MONEY FOR?
SALE
3/15

TO FIGHT THE DRUG WAR.
GOOD FOR YOU. HOW ARE YOU GONNA DO THAT?
COOKIE SALE

BY PROTECTING OUR TURF AGAINST THE OTHER CARTELS.
COOKIE SALE

I LIKE TO REWARD AMBITION.

HI MOM. HI DAD. I JUST CAME BY TO SAY I WON'T BE BRINGING JIMMY OVER TODAY. I HAVE TO TAKE HIM TO HIS SOCCER GAME.
DIDN'T YOU GO TO HIS LAST SOCCER GAME?

YEAH. I GO TO ALL OF HIS GAMES. I HAVEN'T MISSED ONE IN FOUR YEARS.

HAHAHAHAH
3/16

I'M SERIOUS.
YOU MIGHT BE OBSESSIVE.
GET A HOBBY, SWEETIE.

HEY, PIG, THIS IS MY FRIEND, SAL. HE WAS IN PRISON FOR KNIFING SOME GUYS, BUT NOW HE'S IN A REHABILITATION PROGRAM WHERE HE TRIES TO LEARN A NEW SKILL.
DOING WHAT?

I'M SUPPOSED TO RAISE CHICKENS, BUT I HEAR THE STUPID THINGS NEVER LISTEN, SO I DON'T EVEN WANT TO TRY.
OH, C'MON. TAKE A STAB AT IT.
3/17

THAT DIDN'T END WELL.

WHAT DO YOU HAVE THERE, PIG?
FILM SCRIPT. I GOT THREE DIFFERENT PARTS IN THE SAME FILM.
3/18

WHAT DO YOU PLAY?
THREE PRIVATES IN THE ARMY.

GEE, THE DIALOGUE'S PRETTY TRITE. WHAT IF I JUST CHANGE A FEW LINES AND—
PLEASE DON'T TOUCH MY PRIVATE PARTS!

I'LL COME BACK LATER.

WHERE WERE YOU TODAY?
'GENERAL AUTO PARTS.'

DO YOU LIKE IT THERE?
PRETTY MUCH.
3/19

YOU'RE NOT SURE?
I GUESS I LIKE IT IN GENERAL IN GENERAL.

WHAT'D YOU SAY, PRIVATE?
THAT I LIKE IT IN GENERAL IN GENERAL, GENERAL.
STOP

Dis saddest day of my life, Bob.
Me saddest too, Burt.

And me do nuthin wrong.
Me do nuthin wrong neither.

AND NOW WE EES LOSE FREEDOM!
WE EES GOT NO FREEDOM!

3/20

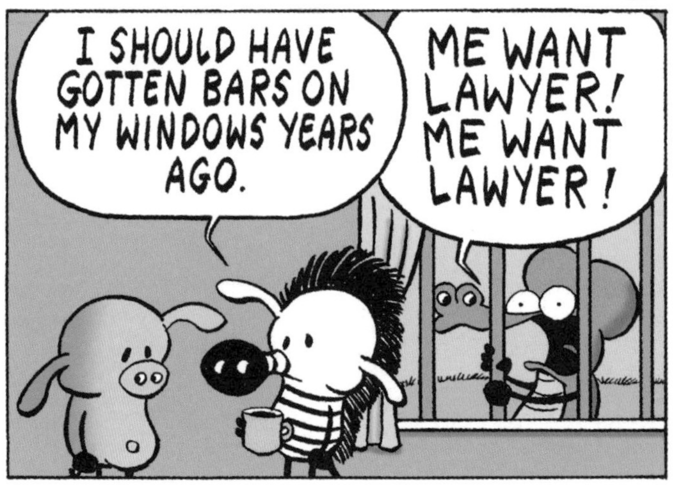
I SHOULD HAVE GOTTEN BARS ON MY WINDOWS YEARS AGO.
ME WANT LAWYER! ME WANT LAWYER!

YOU KNOW, PIG, I'VE BEEN THINKING A LOT ABOUT THE AFTERLIFE LATELY... WHAT DO PIGS THINK HAPPENS TO THEM AFTER THEY DIE?

THEY GET SQUISHED BETWEEN LETTUCE AND TOMATO AND CALLED A B.L.T.
3/21

I MEANT MORE IN THE HEAVENLY SENSE.
A B.L.T. CAN BE PRETTY HEAVENLY.

WHERE YOU OFF TO, GOAT?
NEW DELHI!

DID YOU GET INTO A FIGHT WITH MR. SCHWARTZ?
WHO'S MR. SCHWARTZ?
3/22

THE BUTCHER AT OUR OLD DELI.
LET'S START OVER.

I LIKE IT WHEN HOLLYWOOD MAKES FILMS FOCUSING ON EQUALITY AND THE BROTHERHOOD OF ALL HUMANITY.
WHY IS THAT?
3/23

BECAUSE THEY'RE THE ONLY GROUP THAT DIVIDES ITS OWN PEOPLE INTO A-LISTERS AND EVERYONE ELSE.

I ADMIRE THEIR CHUTZPAH.
BOOOOOO, B-LISTERS, BOOOOOO!

I WANT TO START A BASEBALL LEAGUE FOR AT-RISK YOUTH BUT I DON'T KNOW WHAT IT REQUIRES.
THAT TAKES HELMETS, BATS, GLOVES.
3/24

I DON'T HAVE ALL THAT. WHAT IF I JUST START A DODGEBALL LEAGUE SO THEY CAN TAKE OUT THEIR ANGER IN A SAFE, CONSTRUCTIVE WAY THAT HOPEFULLY DOESN'T LEAD TO MORE VIOLENCE?

THAT JUST TAKES BALLS.

OH, AREN'T YOU CUTE.
WHAT? DODGEBALL REQUIRES BALLS.
BIG ONES, IN FACT.
COMIC STRIP CENSOR

RAT, THE PRESIDENTIAL CANDIDATE
AND SO I WANT TO BUILD A VERY, VERY BIG WALL ON OUR BORDER TO KEEP OUT ALL THE PEOPLE WHO DON'T REPRESENT OUR VALUES AND MAY DO HARM TO OUR COUNTRY.
3/25

SO WHICH SIDE OF THE WALL WILL YOU BE ON?

AND SMART-@## REPORTERS WILL NOT BE TOLERATED.

WELL, WELL, WELL, IT LOOKS LIKE MY RUDE, INCONSIDERATE NEIGHBOR IS ACTUALLY IN A GOOD MOOD TODAY. MAYBE I'LL ACTUALLY SIT NEXT TO YOU.
3/26

THWACK

ALWAYS MASK YOUR TRUE INTENTIONS.

There were none.

So he checked Facebook.

And his fantasy league.

And Snapchat.

And Twitter.

And checked his texts again.

And there was one.

3/27

Are we still on a date?

Elly Elephant vowed to never again date in the smartphone era.

THIS UNIVERSITY DIDN'T LIKE THIS COMEDIAN'S VIEWS ON RELIGION, SO THEY CIRCULATED A PETITION TO STOP HIM FROM SPEAKING.

I THOUGHT THE ANSWER TO SPEECH WE DIDN'T LIKE WAS MORE SPEECH. NOT BANNING THE SPEAKER.
3/28

STOP BEING INTOLERANT.

HEY, NEIGHBOR BOB. THOUGHT I'D STOP BY AND SEE HOW YOU AND YOUR WIFE ARE DOING.
THE ANGELS TOOK HER.

OH, MY GOD. SHE DIED?
NO, NO. THE LOS ANGELES ANGELS GAVE HER A STADIUM JOB.
3/29

I NEED TO FIND A BETTER WAY TO SAY THAT.

HOW GOES YOUR CAMPAIGN FOR PRESIDENT?
GOOD. I HAVE A NEW CAMPAIGN SLOGAN: 'GET UP AND GO.'
GET UP AND GO

AS IN, IF YOU WIN, WE SHOULD ALL WORK TOGETHER ENERGETICALLY TO GET STUFF DONE?
AS IN, IF I LOSE, WE SHOULD ALL GET UP AND GO TO CANADA.
GET UP AND GO
3/30

IF YOU WIN, I *WILL* GO TO CANADA.
MY DRONES WILL TRACK YOU DOWN.
GET UP AND GO

3/31

BOOOO
BOOO
BOOO

'NATURE ABHORS A VACUUM.'
BOOOOO

WE'VE BEEN DATING A LONG TIME, PIGITA. I THINK YOU ARE GREAT. AND I'D LIKE TO MARRY YOU.
OH MY GOD, PIG, REALLY?
4/1

APRIL FOOLS!

SOME APRIL FOOLS JOKES WORK BETTER THAN OTHERS.

THE GOOGLE STREET-VIEW TRUCK CAME DOWN OUR STREET TODAY.
OH, THAT'S THE ONE THAT TAKES PHOTOS SO YOU CAN SEE JUST ABOUT ANY HOUSE IN AMERICA. ISN'T THAT GREAT?

I WAS SUNBATHING IN THE NUDE.
4/2

MAY NO ONE EVER LOOK UP OUR STREET AGAIN.
HEY... SHRINKAGE HAPPENS.

SMITH
1902-1982
Established first state orphanage

WILLIAMS
1911-1966
Philanthropist; Inventor of 12 Life-Saving Vaccines

COOPER
1922-1971
Founder of Metropolitan Art Museum

JONES
1903-1982
Builder of world's largest suspension bridge

4/3

JOHNSON
1968-2016
Had 58 Twitter followers

THE RECENT ONES DEPRESS ME.
WHOA. LOOK AT ALL THIS GUY'S FACEBOOK LIKES.

I CAN NEVER REMEMBER TO TURN OFF THE HEATER WHEN I LEAVE THE HOUSE. SO I STARTED TO REMIND MYSELF WITH STICKY NOTES.
DID THAT WORK?

NO. SO I STARTED PUTTING THE STICKY NOTE ON THE FRONT DOOR SO I'D SEE IT WHEN I WAS LEAVING THE HOUSE.
AND DID THAT WORK?
4/4

NO. SO NOW I'VE DESIGNED THIS HEADBAND THAT HOLDS THE STICKY NOTE RIGHT IN FRONT OF MY FACE.
AND NOW YOU CAN REMEMBER?

REMEMBER WHAT?
GET HELP.

Okay, zeeba... Crocs master helium balloon. Bob gonna float to top of you house. Go down chimney.
HOW WILL YOU MAKE SURE HE DOESN'T JUST FLOAT AWAY?

4/5

You jinx Bob.

HEY, RAT. IT'S ME, GOAT. DO YOU THINK YOU CAN COME OVER AND HELP ME ASSEMBLE A PIECE OF FURNITURE?
LOVE TO. BUT I KNOW NOTHING ABOUT ASSEMBLING FURNITURE.

DO YOU FEIGN IGNORANCE FOR EVERY SINGLE TASK YOU DON'T WANT TO DO?
4/6

THE WORLD IS ON TO ME.

HEY, NEIGHBOR BOB, WHAT ARE YOU UP TO?
I'M THE PRESIDENT OF A NEW COMPANY I JUST FORMED TO FIX DENTED CARS.

HOW IS IT GOING?
GOOD. WE INVENTED THIS NEW TECHNOLOGY WHERE WE SIMPLY PRESS THE DENT BACK OUT FROM THE INSIDE OF THE CAR.

HEY, SINCE I KNOW YOU, COULD I GET A BIT OF A PRESIDENT'S DISCOUNT?
I DON'T KNOW. THAT COULD SET A BAD PRESIDENT PRESS-A-DENT PRECEDENT.
4/7

THIS STRIP NEEDS REPAIRS.

SO, NEIGHBOR BOB, WHAT'S NEW?
I'M TRAINING FOR A TRIATHLON.

I THINK YOU TOLD US THAT FIVE MINUTES AGO. SO HOW'S YOUR FAMILY?
GOOD, BUT NOT AS GOOD AS ME. I'M TRAINING FOR A TRIATHLON.

RIGHT. I KNOW. SO DO YOU WANT A BEER?
CAN'T. I'M TRAINING FOR A TRIATHLON.
4/8

ALL TRIATHLETES SHOULD BE PUNCHED IN THE HEAD.
GOTTA GO. I'M TRAINING FOR A TRIATHLON.

RAT AT THE PRESIDENTIAL DEBATES
CANDIDATE RAT, IF YOU COULD, PLEASE SUM UP WHY YOU ARE RUNNING FOR PRESIDENT IN UNDER FIFTY WORDS.
SURE.

THIS CAMPAIGN IS ABOUT ME, ME, ME, ME, ME, ME, ME, ME, ME, ME, ME, ME, ME, ME, ME, ME, ME, ME, ME, ME, ME, ME, ME, ME, ME, ME, ME, ME, ME, ME, ME, ME, ME, ME, ME, ME.
4/9

YOU CAN STOP NOW.
AND GOD BLESS ME.

ANGRY BOB WAS ANGRY

'THERE ARE SO MANY WAYS TO DIE IN THIS WORLD,' THOUGHT ANGRY BOB. 'AND I DO NOT WANT TO DIE.'

SO ANGRY BOB ATTENDED A SAFETY SEMINAR AT HIS LOCAL FIRE DEPARTMENT AND LEARNED ABOUT VARIOUS FIRE DANGERS. LIKE NOT CLEANING YOUR DRYER'S LINT SCREEN.

AND SO BOB WENT HOME AND DUTIFULLY CLEANED HIS LINT SCREEN.

AND WENT TO SLEEP HAPPY.
ZZZZZZZ

AND THAT NIGHT, THE DISCARDED LINT RE-FORMED ITSELF INTO LINTZILLA.

4/10

AND SUFFOCATED BOB IN HIS SLEEP.

'SO NEVER CLEAN YOUR LINT SCREEN.'
DO NOT TELL PEOPLE THAT.
THERE ARE **SO** MANY WAYS TO ***DIE!***

IT'S BEEN A GREAT TELECONFERENCE, LOU. NOW AS TO THE LAST ITEM ON YOUR AGENDA, HOW 'BOUT WE PUT A PIN IN IT FOR NOW?

HOW 'BOUT I JAM THIS PIN IN YOUR G## FOR USING THAT STUPID EXPRESSION?

4/11

YOWWWWWWWWW
IT'S A POWERFUL DISINCENTIVE.

WHAT ARE YOU DOING?
GOAT'S LAUNDRY. HIS WASHING MACHINE BROKE. HE ASKED ME TO SEPARATE OUT THE WHITES, BUT I DIDN'T.

WHY NOT?
I WON'T TOLERATE RACISM.

4/12

YOU'VE RUINED HIS CLOTHES.
GOOD. RACIST LITTLE UNDERWEAR.

WHAT'S ALL THIS, RAT?
IT'S A VOTING BOOTH THAT I SET UP FOR THE PRESIDENTIAL ELECTION.

BUT IT'S JUST A BRICK WALL.
YEAH. YOU BANG YOUR HEAD AGAINST IT UNTIL YOU FALL UNCONSCIOUS AND MISS THE NEXT FOUR YEARS.

4/13

WHAM
WHAM
WHAM
LOOK. OUR FIRST SATISFIED CUSTOMER.
CAN I BE NEXT?

I HEARD YOU INVITED SOME WOMEN OVER FOR A BIG DANCE PARTY LAST WEEKEND. HOW'D IT GO?
NOT WELL. I DON'T KNOW WHAT IT WAS. MAYBE THE MUSIC.

WHAT'D YOU PLAY?
BRUCE SPRINGSTEEN'S 'NEBRASKA.'

IS CRYING COMMON AT DANCE PARTIES?
4/14

HEY, 'PEARLS' IS GONNA BE PUBLISHED IN A BUNCH OF UNIVERSITY NEWSPAPERS THIS WEEK.
4/15

THAT'S TERRIFIC. UNIVERSITIES HAVE ALWAYS BEEN A BASTION OF FREE SPEECH WHERE YOU CAN TALK ABOUT REMOVED AND REMOVED, EVEN IF YOU'RE A REMOVED WHO LIKES REMOVED OR DOESN'T LIKE REMOVED.

UH...WHAT HAPPENED TO UNIVERSITIES?
WE RAISED A FEW OVER-SENSITIVE NINNIES?
BAN THAT!

HEY, NEIGHBOR BOB, HOW GOES IT?
LAST NIGHT MY WIFE TOLD ME SHE HAD A BIG ANNOUNCEMENT. THEN SHE SAID OUR FAMILY WAS ABOUT TO GROW A LITTLE BIT LARGER.
4/16

WOW. AND WHAT'D YOU SAY?
THAT I THOUGHT WE WERE FAT ENOUGH ALREADY.

I THINK I RUINED A MOMENT.

I STARTED A NEW BUSINESS.

DOING WHAT?
I SELL PEOPLE THEIR OWN CANNING MACHINE AND A SUPPLY OF FRUIT PICKED IN THE AFRICAN SAVANNA.

WHAT KIND OF FRUIT?
MOSTLY BANANAS, WHICH THEY THEN CAN THEMSELVES.

AND WHAT DO THEY DO WITH THEM?
SELL THEM IN COVERED LITTLE POOLSIDE HUTS, BUT SOME CITIES WANT TO BAN THE STRUCTURE.

WHY?
I DUNNO. BUT TO HELP MY CHANCES, I GOT A CELEBRITY PARTNER TO PUT HER NAME ON THE BUSINESS. IT'S THAT WOMAN WHO TURNS THE LETTERS ON 'WHEEL OF FORTUNE.' NOW MAYBE THE CITIES WON'T DO WHAT THEY'RE THREATENING TO DO.
4/17

WHAT ARE CITIES THREATENING TO DO?

BAN A 'VANNA CAN A SAVANNA BANANA' CABANA.

AND JUST LIKE THAT, ANOTHER SUNDAY IS RUINED.

WHAT DO YOU THINK OF ALL THESE WARS GOING ON IN THE MIDDLE EAST?
IT'S A COMPLEX SITUATION. ESPECIALLY WHEN YOU INVOLVE RELIGION AND ALL THEIR SECTS.

THERE'S A LOT OF SEX?
TONS. AND IT'S HARD TO KEEP TRACK OF WHO'S WITH WHOM.

SUDDENLY, I FEEL LIKE VOLUNTEERING.
JUST LIKE THAT? THERE'S NO SUCH THING AS CASUAL SECTS.
4/18

HEY, RAT, I HEARD YOU'RE RUNNING FOR PRESIDENT. WHAT'S YOUR CAMPAIGN CENTERED AROUND?
4/19

SOCIAL ACTIVISM. JUST LIKE GANDHI AND M.L.K., I'M RISKING EVERYTHING TO CHANGE SOCIETY FROM THE GROUND UP.
THAT'S GREAT. SO WHAT DOES THAT INCLUDE? MARCHES? SIT-INS? CIVIL DISOBEDIENCE?

SOMETIMES I CLICK THE 'LIKE' BUTTON ON FACEBOOK.

WOW.
SOMETIMES I EVEN POST A SAD EMOJI.

Hullooo, zeeba neighba... leesten... Crocs find God. Want share gud news.
WHAT'S THE GOOD NEWS?
4/20

Dat one day when you ees die, you go heaven.
WELL, I SUPPOSE THAT IS GOOD NEWS.

AND DAT DAY TOODAY!

I NEED TO STOP ANSWERING THE DOOR.

WHAT ARE YOU LISTEN-ING TO, STEPH?
THIS GREAT STATION. PLAYS ALL THE MUSIC I ALWAYS LOVED IN COLLEGE AND STUFF, LIKE 'GUNS N' ROSES' AND 'NIRVANA.'

OH, YEAH, THAT'S THE 'GOLDEN OLDIES' STATION.

4/21

AND THEN HE CRIED AND LEFT.

WHAT'S THE MATTER WITH YOU?
I HAVE TO GO TO A DINNER PARTY WITH A BUNCH OF ACADEMIC TYPES, AND I'M AFRAID I'M GONNA LOOK STUPID.

JUST TALK LIKE THEY DO AND USE ALL THE BUZZWORDS. YOU KNOW, LIKE 'EXISTENTIAL ANGST,' AND 'PARADIGM SHIFT.'
4/22

AND THANKS FOR LETTING ME USE YOUR BATHROOM, WHERE I RELIEVED MY EXISTENTIAL ANGST WITH A NICE PARADIGM SHIFT.

HEY, STEPH, THIS IS JOHN GLYNN, THE HEAD OF YOUR SYNDICATE, AND I HAVE SOME REAL FAMILY-FRIENDLY, CHUCKLE-FILLED IDEAS FOR YOUR COMIC.
OH. OKAY. WHAT ARE THEY?
4/23

OKAY, WELL, IN THIS FIRST STRIP, THE—
SPLOOSH

FLUSH
HHHHHH HHHHHHHHH HHHHH HHH
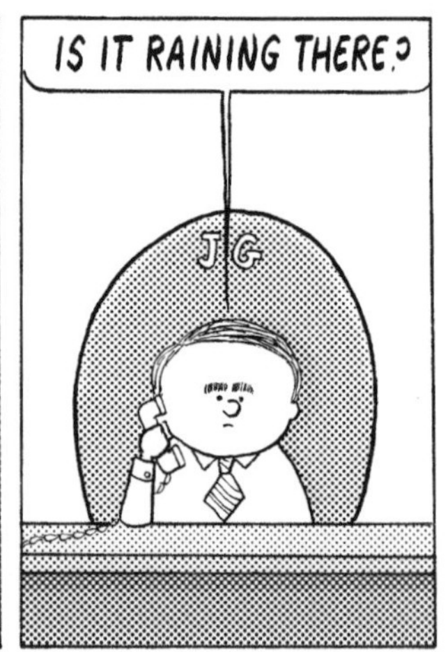
IS IT RAINING THERE?
JG

Stephan Pastis's
Slylock Pearls

Which two scenes are exactly alike?

1 

2 

3 

4 

Answer: Numbers one and two. Numbers one and three. Numbers one and four. Numbers two and three. Numbers two and four. Numbers three and four. (Hey, no one said there were ONLY two.)

Cartoonist Stephan Pastis has been found dead. Which one of the characters is responsible for his death?

TIMMY FAILURE
by Stephan Pastis

Solution: Slylock. He hates puns and stabbed Stephan repeatedly.

Find six differences between these panels.

Answer: (1) Man in first panel is Catholic. Man in second panel is not; (2) First panel drawn ten minutes before the second; (3) Dog in first panel in better mood than dog in second; (4) First panel is above the other; (5) I like the first one more; (6) Other differences.

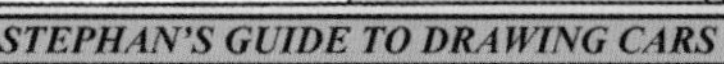
STEPHAN'S GUIDE TO DRAWING CARS

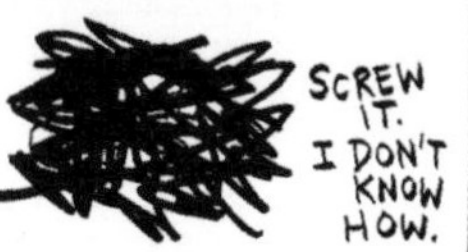
SCREW IT. I DON'T KNOW HOW.

Stephan will receive how many complaints for using the phrase "screw it" in the last panel?

Answer: Oodles

4/24

4/24

HEY, NEIGHBOR BOB, WHATCHA DOING?
TRYING TO READ THIS E-BOOK OUTSIDE. BUT THERE'S TOO MUCH GLARE ON THE SCREEN.
4/25

THAT'S FUNNY. MINE WORKS FINE.
OH, REALLY? WHAT MODEL DO YOU HAVE?

A 'BOOK' BOOK...THE KIND WITH @☆#@☆#@ PAGES... THAT I BOUGHT AT A LOCAL BOOKSTORE...BECAUSE IT'D BE PRETTY @☆#@#@☆ SAD IF OUR LAST REMAINING BOOKSTORE HAD TO SHUT ITS DOORS.

SENSITIVE SUBJECT?
MAY YOUR DAYS BE GLAREY AND BRIGHT.

WHAT ARE YOU WATCHING?
A BUNCH OF LUMBERJACKS WITH LONG SCRAGGLY BEARDS AND FILTHY HELMETS SWINGING AROUND BIG PIECES OF WOOD.

THAT'S A MAJOR LEAGUE BASEBALL GAME.
4/26

I THINK I MISSED A FASHION TREND.

HEY, PIG, THIS IS MY BRITISH FRIEND, ANDREW. HE'S HAPPY BECAUSE HE JUST GOT A FLAT.
WHY IS THAT SOMETHING TO BE HAPPY ABOUT?

BECAUSE I'VE ALWAYS WANTED ONE.
WELL, THEN I'LL JUST TAKE THIS STEAK KNIFE AND SLASH YOUR OTHER THREE TIRES.
4/27

PIG... HE GOT AN APARTMENT!
GOOD, 'CAUSE HE'S NOT GOING ANYWHERE FOR A WHILE.

WHERE'S PIG?
I HIRED HIM AS AN ASSISTANT. SO TODAY HE'S WRITING 'STP' ON ALL MY SOCKS AND UNDERWEAR.

WHAT'S 'STP'?
MY INITIALS, STEPHAN THOMAS PASTIS.
OKAY, STEPH, ALL DONE!
4/28

I SAID 'STP,' NOT 'STD.'
I DON'T HEAR THAT WELL.
OH, YOU WILL SO CHARM THE LADIES.

HEY, PIG, WE'RE GOING TO A ROOFTOP BAR. WANNA COME?
HOLD ON, MOM. GOAT'S ASKING ME SOMETHING.

WHAT'S A ROOFTOP BAR?
IT'S A BAR ON A ROOF. YOU KNOW, NOTHING OVER THE TOP OF YOU. AND THEY SERVE THE BEER OUT OF THESE HUGE CANS. YOU'VE GOT TO SEE IT.

WHERE ARE YOU TWO OFF TO, SON?
A TOPLESS BAR TO SEE SOME HUGE CANS.
4/29

SHE SEEMED LESS THAN EXCITED.

WHAT'S THE MATTER?
I'M ON THE PHONE WITH THE JOHNSONS. THEY WANT TO KNOW WHY WE'RE NOT GOING TO THEIR DINNER PARTY AND I DON'T KNOW WHAT TO TELL THEM.
4/30

WE DON'T LIKE YOU.

THAT WORKED.

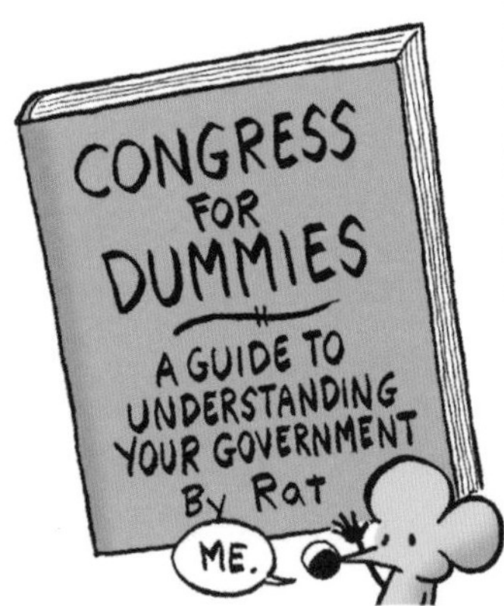
CONGRESS FOR DUMMIES
A GUIDE TO UNDERSTANDING YOUR GOVERNMENT
By Rat
ME.

Congressman parties with big donors.

CRISIS

Congressman goes on T.V.
OUTRAGE!
C-PAN

Congressman holds town hall meetings.
OUTRAGE!
YOU KNOW HE CARES BECAUSE HE'S OUTRAGED.

Congressman attends hearings.
OUTRAGE!!!

5/1

Congressman waits until nobody gives a G#☆#.

Congressman parties with big donors.

AND WE RE-ELECT THEM 90% OF THE TIME.
HEY, SOMEONE HAS TO EMPLOY THESE CHUMPS.
I WILL RE-ELECT THAT CARING CHUMP!
BEER

WHAT ARE YOU DOING, RAT?
CRUSHING THIS MAN BETWEEN TWO AIRLINE SEATS AS A MEANS OF PROTESTING THE CRAMPED SEATING ON AMERIDELTICAN AIRLINES.
5/2

WHY DON'T YOU JUST CONTACT THE C.E.O.?
THIS *IS* THE C.E.O.

I'M MORE DELIGHTED THAN I SHOULD BE.
IF HE WANTS OUT, CHARGE HIM A $50 COMFORT FEE.

HI, GUARD DUCK...WHERE YOU OFF TO SO LATE WITH YOUR 'LIL SCOUT' TROOP?
THE FOREST.

OHH.. ARE YOU GONNA DO A LITTLE CAMPING? MAYBE HAVE A CAMPFIRE?

BURY A BODY.
5/3

HOPE THEY DON'T GET A MERIT BADGE FOR THAT.

LAST YEAR WAS THE 100th ANNIVERSARY OF EINSTEIN'S GENERAL THEORY OF RELATIVITY.
OH, YEAH. RAT EXPLAINED THAT THEORY TO ME.

WHAT DID HE SAY?
THAT THEY'RE ANNOYING AND JUDGMENTAL AND RUIN THE HOLIDAYS.
5/4

THAT'S MY THEORY OF RELATIVES.
SAME THING?
NO.

HEY, LIQUOR STORE LARRY... HOW'S BUSINESS?
GOOD. MY STORE'S NOW BIG ENOUGH THAT THE DISTRIBUTOR GIVES ME MORE LIQUOR THAN I ORDER. AND THE OVERAGE IS FREE.

BECAUSE HE DOESN'T WANT TO LOSE BUSINESS?
YEP. HE DOES IT FOR THE BIG STORES.

THAT'S EXTRA-ORDINARY.
NOT REALLY. I HAVE AVERAGE OVERAGE BEVERAGE LEVERAGE.
5/5

ARE YOU DRINKING AS YOU WRITE THESE?

Dear Mr. Congressman,
I know that now you only represent rich people who give you lots of money.

But I don't have any money.

So here's a crushed donut.
5/6

WE'LL SEE HOW MUCH PULL THAT GIVES ME.

HEY, NEIGHBOR BOB. WHAT ARE YOU DOING?
I'M TIRED OF PEOPLE CRITICIZING ME FOR BEING DEPRESSED, SO I FORMED THIS GROUP. I'M NOW A 'DARN OKAY PERSON THAT IS DEPRESSED.'
THE 'D.O.P.T.I.D.s'

DOES IT RUN IN THE FAMILY?
YEP. MY DAUGHTER HAS IT ALSO. SO SHE'S ONE, TOO.
THE 'D.O.P.T.I.D.s'
5/7

I'M WHAT, DAD?
YOU'RE A 'D.O.P.T.I.D.'
THE 'D.O.P.T.I.D.s'

SHE TOOK IT WORSE THAN I THOUGHT.
THE 'D.O.P.T.I.D.s'

POTATO CHIP PARTY
DING DONG DING DONG

HEY, SOUR CREAM AND ONION! WELCOME!
THANKS, CHEDDAR. WHERE'S BARBECUE?

RIGHT OVER HERE.
SOUR CREAM AND ONION!
BARBECUE!

5/8

COME OVER HERE AND PARTY WITH ME AND COOL RANCH!

SOUR CREAM AND ONION!
COOL RANCH!
PARTY! PARTY! PARTY!
DING DONG DING DONG

WELL, THIS IS A DISORGANIZED MESS.
LET'S DEPART.
LET'S.
LET'S.
LET'S.
LET'S.
LET'S.
LET'S.

STUPID ANAL RETENTIVE PRINGLES.

WHO'S YOUR FRIEND, RAT?
HE'S AN ANGRY BIRD ON DRUGS. HE'S ANGRY 'CAUSE SOME BIGGER BIRDS ATE HIS FRIENDS.

WHY IS HE ON DRUGS?
TO GET THE COURAGE TO COUNTERATTACK. HE WANTS MY HELP IN KNOCKING OFF A COUPLE OF THEM.

SO YOU'RE GONNA KILL TWO BIRDS WITH ONE STONED?

THIS IS A PUN INTERVENTION.
5/9

I THINK THAT THE CAUSE OF MY DEATH WILL BE A PIANO FALLING ON MY HEAD.
THAT'S INTERESTING. DID YOU KNOW THAT 157,000 PEOPLE FROM AROUND THE WORLD WILL DIE ON THE SAME DAY AS YOU?

WOW.
'WOW,' THAT'S A BIG NUMBER?
5/10

WOW, THAT'S A BIG PIANO.

DO YOU HAVE TO WORK AT THE CAFE TOMORROW?
NO. I'M TAKING IT OFF IN HONOR OF THE NATIONAL HOLIDAY.

WHAT NATIONAL HOLIDAY?
GEORGE CARLIN'S BIRTHDAY.
5/11

NOT YET A HOLIDAY.
THEN IT STARTS TOMORROW.
AND TO CELEBRATE, HERE ARE THE SEVEN WORDS YOU CAN'T SAY ON—
SLAP

GOAT, THIS IS MY FRIEND, ED. HE'S AN AIRLINE PILOT.
WOW... I CAN'T BEGIN TO IMAGINE ALL THE COMPLICATED THINGS THAT GO INTO FLYING A COMMERCIAL JET.

I JUST PUSH A BIG BUTTON THAT SAYS 'ZOOMIE ZOOM.'
5/12

I EXPECTED MORE.
WELL, I DO PLAY 'CANDY CRUSH' FOR THE REST OF THE FLIGHT.

Thinking of you...

...Making me a sandwich.
5/13

YOUR HOMEMADE CARDS ARE COUNTER-PRODUCTIVE.
Where Larry sandwich?

WHAT'S YOUR MOTHER DO FOR A LIVING, PIG?

SHE'S A HOMEMAKER.
THAT'S NICE. SO SHE COOKS, CLEANS, DOES THE LAUNDRY?

I MAKE G☆#G☆G# HOMES.
5/14

YOU'RE VERY SEXIST.
LET'S START OVER.
I GOT YOUR LAUNDRY RIGHT HERE, PAL.

HI, GOAT. THIS IS CHARLES. HE JUST MOVED INTO OUR NEIGHBORHOOD.
NICE TO MEET YOU. WHY'D YOU DECIDE TO MOVE HERE?
JUST TO GET AWAY FROM THE PEOPLE WHERE I LIVE. THEY WERENT NICE TO ME.

I'M SORRY TO HEAR THAT.
YEAH, IT WAS PRETTY SAD. BUT NOW I'M ON SOME ANTI-DEPRESSANTS, SO I FEEL A LITTLE BETTER.

ARE YOU MARRIED?
OH NO, NO, NO... I FELL VERY HARD FOR A GIRL YEARS AGO, BUT SHE DIDN'T CARE FOR ME.

SHE DIDN'T BY CHANCE HAVE RED HAIR, DID SHE?
YEAH. WHY?

TAKE OFF YOUR COAT.

5/15

GOOD GRIEF, CHARLIE BROWN.
MIDDLE AGE HAS NOT BEEN KIND.
WANNA KICK A FOOTBALL?

GUYS, MY HEART'S IN THE GAME, BUT MY KNEES, MY ANKLES, THEY JUST CAN'T TAKE IT ANYMORE. SO I'M RETIRING FROM CARTOONING.

MAMBA OUT.
5/16

YOU'RE NOT KOBE BRYANT.
I'M NOT EVEN RETIRING.
MAMBA BREAK MICRO-PHONE.

DO YOU HAVE ANY MORAL CODE THAT YOU USE TO GUIDE YOUR LIFE?
JUST THE GOLDEN RULE.

I'M SURPRISED YOU KNOW IT.
OF COURSE I KNOW IT.

'DO UNTO OTHERS BEFORE THEY GET WIND OF IT AND DO IT UNTO YOU.'
5/17

THAT WASN'T QUITE IT.
I HAD TO BE CLOSE.

5/18

YOU LEARNED HOW TO SCAN PHOTOS INTO THE STRIP.
AND THEY'RE ALL OF MY FACE!
IF HELL HAD WALLPAPER, IT WOULD LOOK LIKE PANEL TWO.

I THINK I WANT TO BE LIKE YOU, L'IL GUARD DUCK, AND PROTECT US AGAINST THE BAD GUYS.
WELL, YOU'D HAVE TO TAKE AN OATH THAT'S A LOT LIKE THE DOCTOR'S OATH.

OH, YEAH? WHAT'S THAT?
'FIRST, DO HARM.'

MAYBE I'LL JUST BE A DOCTOR.
THIS HAS MORE INSTANT GRATIFICATION.
5/19

HEY, STACI...I KNOW WE'VE HAD OUR TOUGH TIMES, BUT WHEN YOU FIRST MET ME, DID YOU EVER FEEL LIKE YOU'D WON THE LOTTERY?

I FELT LIKE I WAS ON 'LET'S MAKE A DEAL' AND WHEN THEY OPENED THE CURTAIN, I GOT A COW.

NO ONE WILL GET THAT REFERENCE!
Moooooooo.
5/20

I'M LOVING THIS BOOK ON THE BRITISH MONARCHY. THIS CHAPTER'S ON THE KINGS AND QUEENS THAT WERE TUDORS.
THEY SOUND NICE.

WHY DO YOU SAY THAT?
THEY HELP YOU WITH ALGEBRA.

TUDORS, NOT TUTORS.
STOP. BEFORE HIS BRAIN EXPLODES.
OHHH, TOOTERS. LIKE HORN BLOWERS.
TOOOOT!
5/21

The council of aliens met at alien headquarters.

We are an advanced race, but that poor race of humans is not. They are sad, silly, and stupid.

So the council of aliens passed a resolution.
We will save the human race from itself.
COUNCIL OF ALIENS

And so, using all of their advanced technology, the aliens constructed their gift to humanity.

And fired it in a rocket to earth.

And thus, I was born.

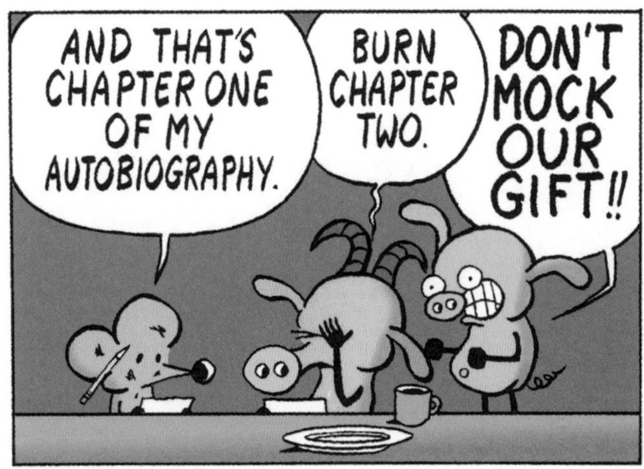
5/22
AND THAT'S CHAPTER ONE OF MY AUTOBIOGRAPHY.
BURN CHAPTER TWO.
DON'T MOCK OUR GIFT!!

WHAT ARE YOU DOING, DAD?
Mom want re-new wedding vows. So me writing what me gonna say.

THAT'S WONDERFUL, DAD. LET'S HEAR IT.
"Me, Larry, ees take wife to have and to hold..."

"For better or worse, or much worse, which ees how it usually ees."
5/23

UH... DAD.
"But being meeserable ees okay, because one day me die."

This strip, which can also be found on p. 78 of this book, was accidentally repeated in newspapers. So we are repeating it here. Because that's how we roll.

DID YOU KNOW THAT NEWSPAPERS CHARGE PEOPLE HUNDREDS OF DOLLARS TO PRINT THE OBITUARIES OF THEIR LOVED ONES?

SO?
SO WE HAVE SPACE IN THE NEWSPAPER.
5/24

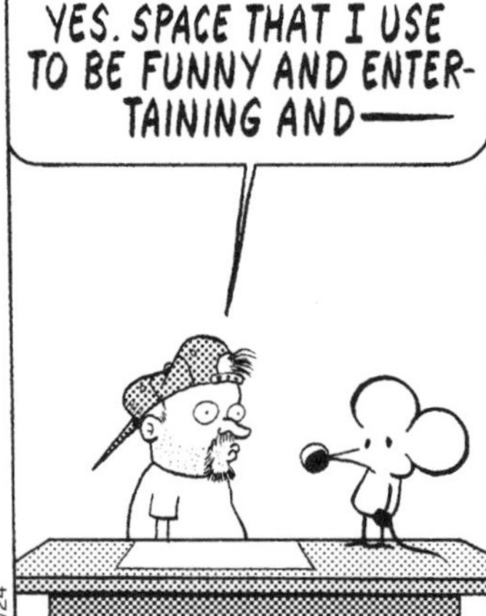

YES. SPACE THAT I USE TO BE FUNNY AND ENTERTAINING AND——

GET RID OF IT.
Jay B. Giblensk
Beloved husband, devo
father. Born in Gdans
Poland in 1952. Died a
his home in Petaluma
last Tuesday evening.
Enjoyed fly fishing and
playing with his dogs,
Bunk, Lester, McNulty
and Stringer Bell. In li
of flowers, donations can
be made to the charity of
your choice.
THIS IS MUCH MORE ENTERTAINING.

YOU WANT SOME OF THIS CINNAMON ROLL?
OH, I USED TO EAT TWO OF THOSE A DAY WHEN I WAS A KID AND NOT GAIN A POUND. BUT NOW, NOT SO MUCH.

WELL, HERE. JUST HAVE ONE BITE THEN.
OKAY.
CHOMP CHOMP CHOMP

I NO LONGER FIT IN THE PANEL.
YOU OWE ME A LIFETIME OF SPIN CLASSES.

WHATCHA READING, GOAT?
A BOOK ABOUT THE DIFFERENT PARTS OF THE BRAIN. YOU KNOW, LIKE THE CEREBRAL CORTEX, THE FRONTAL LOBE, THE HIPPOCAMPUS.

SORRY, PIG...DO YOU KNOW WHAT ALL THAT IS?

THE HIPPOCAMPUS IS WHERE THE HIPPOS GO TO COLLEGE.
5/26

NO.
THEY MUST HAVE VERY LARGE CHAIRS.

HEY, JEF THE CYCLIST. I HEAR THE CITY IS PUTTING BIKE LANES ON EVERY STREET. ISN'T THAT GREAT?
NOT GREAT ENOUGH.

WHAT ELSE DO YOU WANT?
FOR PEOPLE TO CLEAR A SIX-FOOT-WIDE PATH WHEN ANY OF US CYCLISTS IS WALKING AROUND, SO THAT WE DON'T GET YOUR ORDINARINESS ON US.
5/27

I FEEL LIKE I'M SITTING TOO CLOSE.
YOU ARE. CLEAR THE JEF PATH.

I WANT MORE OF EVERYTHING. AND I WANT IT BIGGER AND FASTER.
BUT WHERE DOES THAT ALL END?

WHEN I'VE GOT THE MOSTEST OF THE BIGGEST AND THE FASTEST.
5/28

SO GRAMMAR'S A HIGH PRIORITY?
I WANT THE BESTEST.

HEY, BENNY THE BULL. HOW GOES IT?
GOOD. I'M LEARNING HOW TO IMPRESS WOMEN.

HOW SO?
WITH THIS BOOK, THE 'NOSE-RING DARE.' IT'S ALL THESE CRAZY THINGS YOU CAN DO WITH NOSE RINGS. AND WOMEN LOVE IT.

LOOKS LIKE YOU'VE HIGH-LIGHTED A LOT OF IT.
OH, YEAH. ALL THE IMPORTANT PARTS. BUT THIS IS JUST THE ONE I'VE READ.

YOU HAVE OTHER COPIES?
YEP. I HAVE THIS UNREAD VERSION AS WELL. I KEEP IT IN CASE ANYTHING SHOULD EVER HAPPEN TO THE READ ONE. GOD FORBID.

DUDE, DON'T YOU THINK YOU'RE GOING A LITTLE OVERBOARD? IT'S A STUPID BOOK.
THAT'S RUDE, RAT. BE POLITE.

5/29

OH? WOULD IT BE POLITE OR RUDE OF ME TO STAND ON TOP OF THE READ VERSION?

RUDE! OFF THE READ 'NOSE-RING DARE'!

IT'S NOT EVEN CHRISTMAS.
MY PUNS ARE TIMELESS.

CAN I HELP YOU?
YES, I'M NOAH. I'VE RETURNED TO GATHER EVERYONE WORTHY OF REDEMPTION ONTO MY ARK AND SAVE THEM FROM THE RISING SEAS.

WHO DO YOU HAVE SO FAR?
MY DOG SKIPPY.
5/30

HARD TIMES AHEAD.

WHAT'S WITH ALL THE WATER?
THE OCEANS ARE RISING AND OUR ONLY HOPE IS FOR NOAH TO DEEM US WORTHY OF REDEMPTION AND SAVE US WITH HIS ARK.
5/31

SEE YA. WOULDN'T WANT TO BE YA.

THAT'S DISCOURAGING.

NOAH! NOAH! SAVE US FROM THESE RISING WATERS!
NO CAN DO. ALREADY FILLED THE ARK WITH EVERYONE WHOSE SOUL WAS WORTHY OF SALVATION.

WHO WAS WORTH SAVING?
SCARLETT JOHANSSON.
Hellooo.
6/1

THAT SEEMS BIASED.
PARTY ON THE POOP DECK!

YOU EVER NOTICE HOW SOME ARCHAEOLOGISTS GET ALL THEIR KNOWLEDGE ABOUT CERTAIN CIVILIZATIONS FROM GRAVESITES?
YEAH, SO?

SO I'M GONNA BE BURIED WITH A CHICKEN AND A TOASTER OVEN.
6/2

GOOD FOR YOU.
DID THIS CIVILIZATION LOVE TOAST? OR CHICKENS? OR DID THE CHICKENS LOVE TOAST?

YOUR FURNITURE DOESN'T COME WITH A LIST OF ALL THE PEOPLE WHO WORKED ON PUTTING IT TOGETHER. NOR DO YOUR SHOES. OR YOUR SHIRT. OR YOUR CAR. OR YOUR CARPET.
SO?

SO WHY DO MOVIES?
6/3

SOMETIMES YOU STUMP EVEN ME.
ATTENTION: GAFFERS... I DO NOT NEED YOUR NAME!

LOOK AT THAT BIRD SITTING ON THE AUTOMATIC SPRINKLER.
YEAH, THAT'S BENNY THE FLIGHTLESS ROBIN.

WHY'S HE JUST SITTING THERE?
HE'S HOPING THAT ONE DAY THE SPRINKLER WILL TURN ON AND POP HIM UP INTO THE AIR, GIVING HIM THE ILLUSION OF FLIGHT.

THAT, AND IT'S CHEAPER THAN A BIDET.
6/4

THAT'S BOTH SAD *AND* REVOLTING.
A LITTLE PRIVACY, PLEASE.

I HEAR YOU WENT TO THE DODGERS/ GIANTS GAME. WHAT WAS THE SCORE?
GIANTS ONE. DODGERS TWO.
HOW CAN THEY BOTH WIN?
THEY DIDN'T. I SAID THE GIANTS HAD ONE.
AND THE DODGERS, TOO?
RIGHT.
THAT MAKES NO SENSE. DID YOU AT LEAST HAP-PEN TO SEE HOW MANY RUNS THE PADRES SCORED IN THEIR GAME?
FOUR.
FOR MY BET. I HAVE BIG MONEY ON THEM.
THEN I HOPE THAT'S THE NUM-BER YOU NEEDED.
WHAT'S THE NUMBER I NEEDED?
I JUST TOLD YOU. IF YOU DON'T BE-LIEVE ME, ASK MY GERMAN FRIEND, HANS.
FINE. DO YOU KNOW HOW MANY RUNS THE PADRES SCORED?
NEIN.
YOU SAID IT WAS FOUR SOME-THING.
YOU SAID IT WAS FOR SOME-THING.
6/5
DUDE, JUST GIMME THE RIGHT DODGERS/GIANTS SCORE AND I'LL BUY YOU YOUR STUPID LUNCH, UNLESS YOU ALREADY HAD FOOD AT THE GAME.
ATE NOTHING.
WHO HAD NOTHING?
ME.
AHHHHHHHH
I WAS TOO UPSET THE DODGERS HAD WON.

Pearls Before Swine is distributed internationally by Andrews McMeel Syndication.

Andrews McMeel Publishing
a division of Andrews McMeel Universal
1130 Walnut Street, Kansas City, Missouri 64106

www.andrewsmcmeel.com

17 18 19 20 21 SDB 10 9 8 7 6 5 4 3 2 1

ISBN: 978-1-4494-8380-7

Library of Congress Control Number: 2017936767

Pearls Before Swine can be viewed on the Internet at
www.pearlscomic.com

These strips appeared in newspapers from September 7, 2015 to June 5, 2016.